A Valiant Igr

Vol. 1

Mary Angela Dickens

Alpha Editions

This edition published in 2024

ISBN : 9789362096562

Design and Setting By
Alpha Editions
www.alphaedis.com
Email - info@alphaedis.com

As per information held with us this book is in Public Domain.
This book is a reproduction of an important historical work. Alpha Editions uses the best technology to reproduce historical work in the same manner it was first published to preserve its original nature. Any marks or number seen are left intentionally to preserve its true form.

Contents

CHAPTER I .... - 1 -
CHAPTER II .... - 10 -
CHAPTER III .... - 14 -
CHAPTER IV .... - 21 -
CHAPTER V .... - 27 -
CHAPTER VI .... - 33 -
CHAPTER VII .... - 38 -
CHAPTER VIII .... - 44 -
CHAPTER IX .... - 54 -
CHAPTER X .... - 65 -
CHAPTER XI .... - 76 -
CHAPTER XII .... - 87 -
CHAPTER XIII .... - 92 -
CHAPTER XIV .... - 99 -

CHAPTER I

"My dear Mamma,

"I hope you are quite well. I am quite well, and Smut is quite well. Her tail is very fat. I hope papa is quite well. I have a box of soldiers. The captain has a horse. Uncle Richard gave them to me. There is a hole in the horse, and he sticks in tight. Auntie is quite well, and so is nurse, and so is cook.

"I am, your loving Son,
"Julian."

It was the table d'hôte room of one of the best hotels in Nice; a large room, gay and attractive, according to its kind, as fresh paint, bright decoration, and expanse of looking-glass could make it. From end to end were ranged small tables, varying in size but uniform in the radiant spotlessness of their white cloths, and the brightness of their silver, china, or glass; and to and fro between the tables, and from the tables to the door, moved active waiters, whose one aim in life seemed to be the anticipation of the wishes of the visitors for whose pleasure alone they apparently existed.

It was early, and *déjeuner* proper was hardly in full swing as yet. But a good many of the tables were occupied, and a subdued hum of conversation pervaded the air; a hum compounded of the high-pitched chatter of American women and the quick, eager volubility of French tongues, backed by a less pronounced but perfectly perceptible undercurrent of German and English; the whole diversified now and then by a light laugh.

The sounds were subdued because the room was large and sparsely filled, but they were gay. The smiling alacrity of the waiters was apparently at once a symptom of, and a subtle tribute to, the humour of the hour. There were sundry strongly-marked faces here and there among the little groups; middle-aged men to whom neither ambition nor care could have been empty words; middle-aged women with lines about their faces not lightly come by; young girls with the vague desire and unrest of youth; young men with its secrets and its aspirations. But all individuality of care, anxiety, or desire seemed to be in abeyance for the time being; enjoyment—somewhat conventional, well-dressed enjoyment, of the kind that rather covers up trouble as not "the thing" than disperses it—was evidently the order of the day. It was within three days of the carnival, and the visitors who were crowding into Nice came one and all with fixedly and obviously light-hearted intention.

The link between the little letter—not little by any means in a material sense, since its capitals sprawled and staggered over a large sheet of foreign letter paper—and the smart, pleasure-seeking atmosphere of the Nice table d'hôte room, was a woman who sat at a little table by one of the open windows. And she was much more easily to be identified, arguing from her appearance and manner, with her present surroundings than with the images conjured up by the blotted letter in her hand. She was a small woman, with a very erect little figure, the trimness of which was accentuated by the conventional perfection of the dress she wore; it was not such a dress as would commend itself to the fashionable woman of to-day—at that date, eighteen hundred and seventy-two, tailor-made garments for ladies were not—but it had won a glance of respect, nevertheless, from every woman in the room in the course of the few minutes which had elapsed since its wearer had entered. Her hair was fair; very plentiful and very fashionably dressed. Her eyes were blue; her colouring pale. If she had had no other claims on a critic's attention, no more marked characteristics, she might have been called rather pretty. She was rather pretty, as a matter of fact, but her prettiness was dwarfed, and put out of sight by the stronger influence of her manner and expression.

As she sat there reading her letter, neither moving nor speaking, she was stamped from head to foot—as far as externals went—as one of a type of woman which commands more superficial homage than perhaps any other—the woman of the world. The self-possession, the quiet, unquestioning assurance, even the superficiality of her expression in its total absence of intellectuality or emotionalism, spoke to character; the narrow character, truly, which is cognisant only of shallow waters, knows them, and reigns in them. But it was a noticeable feature about her that even this character had gone to the accentuation of the type in her. As to her age, it would have been extremely difficult to guess it from her appearance. Her face was quite unworn—evidently such emotions as she had known had gone by no means deep—and yet it was not young; there was too much knowledge of the world about it for youthfulness. As a matter of fact, she was twenty-six years old. She was sitting alone at the little table by the window, and her perfect freedom from nervousness, or even consciousness of the admiring glances cast at her, emphasized her perfect self-possession.

A waiter, smiling and assiduous even beyond the smiling assiduity with which he had waited at other tables, appeared with her breakfast, and as he arranged it on the table, she replaced the blotted letter in its envelope with a certain lingering touch that was apparently quite unconscious, and contrasted rather oddly with her self-possessed face.

The envelope was addressed in a woman's writing to "Mrs. William Romayne, Hôtel Florian, Nice." It was one of a pile, and she took up the others and looked them through. They all bore the same name.

"There are no letters for Mr. Romayne?" she said to the waiter carelessly.

The voice was rather thin, and, as would have been expected from her face, slightly unsympathetic, but it was refined and well modulated. Her French was excellent.

The waiter thus questioned showed a letter—a business-like looking letter in a blue envelope—which he had brought in on his tray; and presented it with a torrent of explanation and apology. It had arrived last night, before the arrival of monsieur and madame, and with unheard-of carelessness, but with quite amazing carelessness indeed, it had been placed in a private sitting-room ordered by another English monsieur, who had arrived only this morning. By the valet of this English monsieur it had been given to the waiter this moment only; by the waiter it was now given to madame with ten million desolations that such an accident should have occurred. Monsieur had seemed so anxious for letters on his arrival! If madame would have the goodness to explain!

Madame stopped the flood of protestations with a little gesture. However it might affect monsieur, the accident did not appear to disturb her greatly. Indeed, it was inconceivable that she should be easily ruffled.

"Let Mr. Romayne have the letter at once," she said, "and send him also a cup of coffee and an English newspaper!"

The waiter signified his readiness to do her bidding with the greatest alacrity, took the letter from her with an apologetic bow, laid by her side a newspaper for madame's own reading, as he said, and retired. Left once more alone, madame proceeded to breakfast in a dainty, leisurely fashion, ignoring the newspaper for the present, and drawing from the envelope in which she had replaced the childish little epistle, a second letter. It was a long one, and she read it placidly as she went on with her breakfast.

"MY DEAR HERMIA," it ran, "Julian has just accomplished the enclosed with a great deal of pride and excitement. The wild scrawls that occur here and there were the result of imperative demands on his part to be allowed to write 'all by himself'! The dear pet is very well, and grows sweeter every day, I believe. You were to meet Mr. Romayne at Mentone, on the second, I think he said, and to go on to Nice the next day, so I hope you will get this soon after you arrive there. I hope the change will do Mr. Romayne good. He came here to see Julian yesterday, and I did not think him looking well, nor did father. He only laughed when father told him so. We were so glad to get your last letter. You are not a very good correspondent, are you? But, of course, you were going out a great deal in Paris and had not much time for writing. You seem to have had a delightful time there.

"Dennis Falconer came back last week. He has been away nearly a year, you know. He is very brown, and has a long beard, which is rather becoming. The

Royal Geographical are beginning to think rather highly of him, father is told, and he will probably get something important to do before long. Father wanted him to come and stay here, but he has gone back to his old chambers. Not very cousinly of him, I think!

"You don't say whether you are coming to London for the season? I asked Mr. Romayne, but he said he did not know what your plans were. I do so hope you will come, though I am afraid I should not be pleased if the spirit should move you to settle down in England and demand Julian! However, I suppose that is not very likely?

"With much love, dear Hermia,
"Your very affectionate Cousin,
"FRANCES FALCONER."

Mrs. Romayne finished the letter, which she had read with leisurely calm, as though her interest in it was by no means of a thrilling nature, and then opened and glanced through, the others which were waiting their turn. They were of various natures; one or two came from villas about Nice, and consisted of more or less pressing invitations; one was from a well-known leader of society in Rome—a long, chatty letter, which the recipient read with evident amusement and interest. There were also one or two bills, at which Mrs. Romayne glanced with the composure of a woman with whom money is plentiful.

Breakfast and correspondence were alike disposed of at last, and by this time the room was nearly full. The laughter and talk was louder now, the atmosphere of gaiety was more accentuated. Outside in the sunshine in the public gardens a band was playing. Mrs. Romayne was alone, it is true, and her voice consequently added nothing to the pervading note, but her presence, solitary as it was, was no jarring element. She was not lonely; her solitude was evidently an affair of the moment merely; she was absolutely in touch with the spirit of the hour, and no laughing, excited girl there witnessed more eloquently or more unconsciously to the all-pervading dominion of the pleasures of life than did the self-possessed looking little woman, to whom its pleasures were also its businesses—the only businesses she knew.

She had gathered her letters together, and was rising from her seat with a certain amount of indecision in her face, when a waiter entered the room and came up to her. "Some ladies wishing to see madame were in the salon," he said, and he handed her as he spoke a visiting-card bearing the name, "Lady Cloughton." Underneath the name was written in pencil, "An unconscionable hour to invade you, but we are going this afternoon to La Turbie, and we hope we may perhaps persuade you to join us."

"The ladies are in the salon, you say?" said Mrs. Romayne, glancing up with the careless satisfaction of a woman to whom the turn of events usually does bring satisfaction; perhaps because her demands and her experience are alike of the most superficial description.

"In the salon, madame," returned the waiter. "Three ladies and two gentlemen."

He was conducting her obsequiously across the room as he spoke, and a moment later he opened the door of the salon and stood aside to let her pass in.

A little well-bred clamour ensued upon her entrance; greetings, questions and answers as between acquaintances who had not met for some time, and met now with a pleasure which seemed rather part and parcel of the gaiety to which the atmosphere of the dining-room had witnessed than an affair of the feelings. All Mrs. Romayne's five visitors were apparently under five-and-thirty, the eldest being a man of perhaps three or four-and-thirty, addressed by Mrs. Romayne as Lord Cloughton; the youngest a pretty girl who was introduced by the leader of the party, presumably Lady Cloughton, herself quite a young woman, as "my little sister." They were all well-dressed; they were all apparently in the best possible spirits, and bent upon enjoyment; and gay little laughs interspersed the chatter, incessantly breaking from one or the other on little or no apparent provocation. Eventually Lady Cloughton's voice detached itself and went on alone.

"We heard you were here," she said, "from a man who is staying here. We are at the Français, you know. And we said at once, 'Supposing Mrs. Romayne is not engaged for to-morrow'—so many people don't come, you see, until the day before the carnival, and consequently, of course, one has fewer friends and fewer engagements, and this week is not so full, don't you know—'supposing she has no engagement for to-morrow,' we said, 'how pleasant it would be if she would come with us to La Turbie.' We have to make Mr. Romayne's acquaintance, you know. So charmed to have the opportunity! I hope he is well?"

"Fairly well, thanks," replied his wife. "He has been in London all the winter—his business always seems to take him to the wrong place at the wrong time—and either the climate or his work seems to have knocked him up a little. He seems to have got into a shocking habit of sitting up all night and staying in bed all day. At least he has acted on that principle during the week we have been together. He is actually not up yet."

Mrs. Romayne smiled as she spoke; her husband's "shocking habits" apparently sat very lightly on her; in fact, there was something singularly disengaged and impersonal in her manner of speaking of him, altogether. Her visitor received her smile with a pretty little unmeaning laugh, and went on with much superficial eagerness:

"He may, perhaps, be up in time for our expedition, though! We thought of starting in about two hours' time. They say the place is perfectly beautiful at this time of year. Perhaps you know it."

"No," returned Mrs. Romayne. "Oddly enough I have never been to Nice before. I have often talked of wintering here, but I have always eventually gone somewhere else! Are you here for the first time?" she added, turning to the young man, whom she had received as Mr. Allan, and who evidently occupied the position of mutual acquaintance between herself and her other visitors. He was answering her in the affirmative when Lord Cloughton struck in with a cheery laugh.

"He's been here two days, and he has come to the conclusion that Nice is a beastly hole, Mrs. Romayne!" he said. "This afternoon's expedition is really a device on our part for cheering him up. He let himself be persuaded into putting some money into a new bank, and the new bank has smashed. Have you seen the papers? Now, Allan hasn't lost much, fortunately; it isn't that that weighs upon him. But he is oppressed by a sense of his own imbecility, aren't you, old fellow?"

The young man laughed, freely enough.

"Perhaps I am," he said. "So would you be, Cloughton, wouldn't he, Mrs. Romayne? And don't tell me you wouldn't have done the same, because any fellow would, in my place. However, if Mrs. Romayne is more likely to join us this afternoon if the proceedings are presented to her in the light of a charity, I'm quite willing to pose as an object! Take pity on me, Mrs. Romayne, do!"

"I shan't pity you," answered Mrs. Romayne lightly. "You don't seem to me to be much depressed, and your misfortunes appear to be of your own making. But I shall be delighted to go with you this afternoon," she continued, turning to Lady Cloughton. "And I feel sure that Mr. Romayne will also be delighted."

"That is quite charming of you!" exclaimed Lady Cloughton, rising as she spoke. "Well, then, I think if we were to call for you—yes, we will call for you in two hours from now. So glad you can come! The little boy quite well? So glad. In two hours, then! Au revoir."

There was a flutter of departure, a chorus of bright, meaningless, last words, and Mrs. Romayne stood at the head of the great staircase, waving her hand in farewell as her visitors, with a last backward glance and parting smiles and gestures, disappeared from view. She stood a moment watching some people in the hall below, whose appearance had struck her at dinner on the previous evening, and as she looked idly at them she saw a man come in—an Englishman, evidently just off a journey, and "not a gentleman" as she decided absently—and go up to a waiter who was standing in the dining-room doorway. The Englishman evidently asked a question and then another and another, and finally the waiter glanced up the stairs to where Mrs. Romayne stood carelessly watching, and obviously pointed her out to his interlocutor, asking a question in his turn. The Englishman, after looking quickly in Mrs. Romayne's direction, shook his head in answer and walked into the dining-room.

With a vague feeling of surprise and curiosity Mrs. Romayne turned and moved away. She retraced her steps, evidently intending to go upstairs, but as she passed the open door of the drawing-room she hesitated; her eyes caught by the bright prospect visible through the open windows which looked out over the public gardens and the blue Mediterranean; her ears caught by the sounds from the band still playing outside. She re-entered the room, crossed to the window and stood there, looking out with inattentive pleasure, the dialogue she had witnessed in the hall quite forgotten as she thought of her own affairs. She thought of the immediate prospects of the next few weeks; wholly satisfactory prospects they were, to judge from her expression. She thought of the letters she had received that morning, mentally answering the invitations she had received. She thought of the acquaintances who had just left her, and of the engagement she had made for that afternoon; and then, as if the necessity for seeing her husband on the subject had by this means become freshly present to her, she turned away from the window and went out of the room and up the staircase. On her way she chanced to glance down into the hall and noticed the Englishman to whom the waiter had pointed her out, leaning in a reposeful and eminently stationary attitude against the entrance. She would ask who he was, she resolved idly. She went on until she came to a door at the end of a long corridor, outside which stood a dainty little pair of walking shoes and a pair of man's boots. She glanced at them and lifted her eyebrows slightly—a characteristic gesture—and then opened the door.

It led into a little dressing-room, from which another doorway on the left led, evidently, into a larger room beyond. The glimpse of the latter afforded by the partly open door showed it dim and dark by contrast with the light outside; apparently the blind was but slightly raised. There was no sunshine in the dressing-room, either, though it was light enough; and as Mrs. Romayne went in and shut the door she seemed to pass into a silence that was almost oppressive. The band, the strains of which had reached her at the very threshold, was not audible in the room; in shutting the door she seemed to shut out all external sounds, and within the room was absolute stillness.

The contrast, however, made no impression whatever upon Mrs. Romayne. She was by no means sensitive, evidently, to such subtle influence. She glanced carelessly through the doorway into the dim vista of the bedroom beyond, and going to the other end of the dressing-room knelt down by a portmanteau, and began to search in it with the uncertainty of a woman whose packing is done for her by a maid. She found what she wanted; sundry dainty adjuncts to out-of-door attire, one of which, a large lace sunshade, required a little attention. She took up an elaborate little case for work implements that lay on the table, and selected a needle and thread, and a thimble; and perhaps the dead silence about her oppressed her a little, unconsciously to herself, for she hummed as she did so a bar or two of the waltz she had shut out as she shut the door. Then with the needle moving deftly to and fro in her white, well-shaped hands, she moved down the dressing-room, and standing in the light for the sake of her work, she spoke through the doorway into the still, dark bedroom.

"The Cloughtons have been here, William," she said. "The people I met in Rome this winter; I think I told you, didn't I? They wanted us to go to La Turbie with them this afternoon, and I said we would. That is to say, I only answered conditionally for you, of course. Will you go?"

There was no answer, no sound of any kind. Not so much as a stir or a rustle to indicate that the sleep of the man hidden in the dimness beyond—and only sleep surely could account for his silence—was even broken by the words addressed to him. Yet the voice which proceeded from the serene, well-appointed little figure standing in the sombre light of the dressing-room, with its attention more or less given to the trivial work in its hands, was penetrating in its quality, though not loud.

Mrs. Romayne paused a moment, listening. Then, with that expressive movement of her eyebrows, she went back again to the dressing-table she had left, took up a little pair of scissors which were necessary to give the finishing touch to her work, gave that finishing touch with careless deliberation, studied the effect with satisfaction, and then laid down the sunshade, and returned to the doorway into the bedroom. She stood on the threshold this time, and the darkness before her and the sombre light behind her seemed to meet upon her figure; the silence and stillness all about her seemed to claim even the space she occupied.

"William!" she said crisply. "William!"

Again there was no answer; no sound or stir of any sort or kind. And for the first time the silence seemed to strike her. She moved quickly forward into the dimness.

"William! Are you asleep——"

Her eyes had fallen on the bed, and she stopped suddenly. For it was empty. She paused an instant, and in that instant the silence seemed to rise and dominate the atmosphere as with a grim and mighty presence, before which everything shallow or superficial sank into insignificance. All that was typical and conventional about the woman standing in the midst of the stillness, arrested by she knew not what, suddenly seemed to stand out jarring and incongruous, as though unreality had been met and touched into self-revelation by a great reality. Then it subsided altogether, and only the simplest elements of womanhood were left—the womanhood common to the peasant and the princess—as the wife took two or three quick steps forward. She turned the corner of the bed that hid the greater part of the room from her, and then staggered back with a sharp cry. At her feet, partly dressed, there lay the figure of the man to whom she had been talking; his right hand, dropped straight by his side, clenched a revolver; his face—a handsome face probably an hour ago—was white and fixed; his eyes were glassy. On the floor beside him lay an open letter—a letter written on blue paper.

William Romayne was asleep indeed. His wife might tear at the bell-rope; the hotel servants might hurry and rush to and fro; even the recently-arrived Englishman might render his assistance. But it was all in vain. William Romayne was beyond their reach.

CHAPTER II

THE long railway journey from Paris to Nice was nearly over. The passengers, jaded and tired out, for the most part, after a night in the train, were beginning to rouse to a languid interest in the landscape; to become aware that dawn and the uncomfortable and unfamiliar early day had some time since given place to a fuller and maturer light; and to consult their watches, reminding themselves—or one another, as the case might be—that they were due at Nice at twelve-fifteen.

Alone in one of the first-class carriages was a passenger who had accepted the situation with the most matter-of-fact indifference from first to last. He had made his arrangements for the night, with the skill and deliberation of an experienced traveller; and as the morning advanced he had composed himself, as comfortably as circumstances permitted, in a corner of his carriage, now and then casting a keen, comprehensive glance at the country through which he was being carried. These glances, however, were evidently instinctive and almost unconscious. For the most part he gazed straight before him with a preoccupied frown and a grave and anxious expression in marked contrast with his physical imperturbability. He was a man of apparently three or four-and-thirty; tall; rather lean than thin; and very muscular-looking. His face, and the right hand from which he had pulled off the glove, were bronzed a deep red-brown, and he wore a long brown beard; but he was not otherwise remarkable-looking. His eyes, indeed, were very keen and steady, but the rest of his face conveyed the impression that he owed these characteristics rather to trained habits of material observation than to general intellectual depths; the mouth was firm and strong, but neither sensitive nor sympathetic, and the straight, well-cut nose was as distinctly too thin as the rather high forehead was too narrow. On a much-worn travelling-bag on the seat beside him, was the name Dennis Falconer.

The train steamed slowly into the station at Nice at last; the traveller stepped out on to the platform, and the shade of grave preoccupation which had touched him seemed to descend on him more heavily and all-absorbingly as he did so. He was walking down the platform, looking neither to the right nor the left, when he was stopped by a quick exclamation from a little wiry man with a shrewd, clever face who had just come into the station.

"Falconer, as I'm alive," he cried. "Well met, my boy!"

The gravity of the younger man's face relaxed for the moment into a smile of well-pleased astonishment.

"Dr. Aston!" he exclaimed. "Why, I was thinking of looking you up in London! I'd no idea you were abroad!"

The other man laughed, a very pleasant, jovial laugh.

"I'm taking a holiday," he said. "I don't know that I've any particular right to it! But I don't know these places, and I took it into my head that I should like to have a look at a carnival in Nice. And you, my boy? Just back from Africa, you are, I know. You've come for the carnival by way of a change, eh?"

Falconer's face altered.

"No!" he said gravely, and with a good deal of restraint. "I've not come for pleasure. Very much the reverse, I'm sorry to say."

He paused, apparently intending to say no more on the subject. But the keen, kindly interest in his hearer's face, or something magnetic about the man, influenced him in spite of himself.

"I don't know whether the facts about this bank business are known here yet," he said, "but if they are you'll understand, Aston, when I tell you that I and my old uncle are the only male relations of William Romayne's wife."

A quick flash of grave intelligence passed across Dr. Aston's face. He hesitated, and glanced dubiously at the younger man.

"When did you leave London?" he said abruptly.

"Yesterday morning," was the somewhat surprised reply.

"You've come in good time, my boy," said Dr. Aston very gravely. "Mrs. Romayne wants a relation with her if ever she did in her life. Was her husband ever a friend of yours, Dennis?"

"I have never met him. I know very little even of his wife. What is it, doctor?"

"William Romayne shot himself yesterday morning!"

A short, sharp exclamation broke from Falconer, and then there was a moment's total silence between the two men as the sudden, unspeakable horror in Falconer's face resolved itself into a shocked, almost awestruck gravity.

"I am thankful to have met you," he said at last in a low, stern voice; "and I am more than thankful that I came."

He held out his hand as he spoke, as though what he had heard impelled him to go on his way, and Dr. Aston wrung it with warm sympathy.

"We shall meet again," he said. "Let me know if I can be of any use. I am staying at the Français."

Grave and stern, but not apparently shaken or rendered nervous by the news he had heard, or by the prospect of the meeting before him, as a sympathetic or emotional man must have been, Dennis Falconer strode out of the station. Grave and stern he reached his destination, and enquired for Mrs. Romayne. His question was answered by the proprietor himself, supplemented by half-audible ejaculations from attendant waiters, in a tone in which sympathetic interest, familiarity, and even a certain amount of resentment were inextricably blended.

Monsieur would see Madame Romayne—*cette pauvre madame*, of a demeanour so beautiful, yes, even in these frightful circumstances, so beautiful and so distinguished? Monsieur had but just arrived from England—monsieur had then perhaps not heard? Monsieur was aware? He was a kinsman of madame? Monsieur would then doubtless appreciate the so great inconvenience occasioned, the hardly-to-be-reckoned damage sustained by one of the first hotels in Nice, by the event? Monsieur would see madame at once? But yes, madame was visible. There was, in fact, a monsieur with her even now—an English monsieur from the English Scotland Yard. Madame had sent—— But monsieur was indeed in haste.

Monsieur left no possibility of doubt on that score. The waiter, told off by a wave of the proprietor's hand on the vigorous demonstration to that effect evoked by the mention of the monsieur from Scotland Yard, had to hasten his usual pace considerably to keep ahead of those quick, firm footsteps, and it was almost breathlessly that he at last threw open a door at the end of a long corridor.

"Mr. Romayne's name is public property in connection with the affair, then, in London, since yesterday morning?"

The words, spoken in a hard, thin, woman's voice, came to Falconer's ear as the door opened; and the waiter's announcement, "A kinsman of madame," passed unheeded as he moved hastily forward into the room.

It was a small private sitting-room, evidently by no means the best in the hotel. With his back to the door stood a young man in an attitude of professional calm, rather belied by a certain nervous fingering of the hat he held, which seemed to say that he found his position a somewhat embarrassing one. Facing him, and indirectly facing the door, stood Mrs. Romayne.

She was dressed in black from head to foot, but the gown she wore was one that she had had in her wardrobe—very fashionably made, with no trace of mourning about it other than its hue.

Emphasized, perhaps, by the incongruity of her conventional smartness, but a result of the past twenty-four hours independent of any such emphasis, all the more salient points of her demeanour of the day before seemed to be accentuated into hardness. Her perfect self-possession, as she faced the young man before her—it was the man she had noticed on the previous morning questioning the waiter—was hard; her perfect freedom from any touch of emotion or agitation was hard; her face, a little sharpened and haggard, and reddened slightly about the eyelids, apparently rather from want of sleep than from tears, was very hard; her eyes, brighter than usual, and her rather thin mouth, were eloquent of bitterness, rather than desolation, of spirit.

She turned quickly towards the door as Falconer entered, and looked at him for an instant with an unrecognising stare. Then, as he advanced to her without speaking, and with outstretched hand, something that was almost a spasm of comprehension passed across her face, settling into a stiff little society smile.

"It is Dennis Falconer, isn't it?" she said, holding out her hand to him. "I ought to have known you at once. I am very glad to see you."

"My uncle thought—— We decided yesterday morning——"

Dennis Falconer hesitated and stopped. He was thrown out of his reckoning, taken hopelessly aback, as it were, by something so entirely unlike what he had expected as was her whole bearing; though, indeed, he had been quite unconscious of expecting anything. But Mrs. Romayne remained completely mistress of the situation.

"It is very kind of you," she said, with the same hard composure. "It was very kind of my uncle." She hesitated, hardly perceptibly, and then said, the lines about her mouth growing more bitter, "You have heard?"

Falconer bowed his head in assent, and she turned toward the young man, who had drawn a little apart during this colloquy.

"This gentleman comes from Scotland Yard," she said. "Perhaps you will be so kind as to go into matters with him. I do not understand business or legal details. Mr. Falconer will represent me," she added to the young man, who bowed with an alacrity that suggested, as did his glance at Falconer, that the prospect of conferring with a man rather than a woman was a distinct relief to him. Then, before Falconer's not very rapid mind had adjusted itself to the situation, she had bowed slightly to the young man and left the room.

CHAPTER III

THREE days before, the name of William Romayne had been widely known and respected throughout Europe as the name of a successful and distinguished financier. Now, it was the centre of a nine-days' wonder as the name of a master swindler, detected.

A bank, established in London within the last twelve months in connection with a company offering an exceptionally high rate of interest, had suddenly suspended payment. The circumstances were so ordinary, and the explanation offered so plausible, that at first no suspicion of underhand dealings presented itself. It was in connection with the first whispers—which ran like wildfire through financial London—of something beneath the surface, that it first became known that William Romayne had some connection, as yet undefined by rumour, with the bank in question; a fact hitherto quite unknown. The whispers grew with rapidity which was almost incredible even to the whisperers, into a definite and authentic shout of accusation; and with the exposure of an outline of such daring and ingenious fraud as had not been perpetrated for many a day, another fact had become public property. The exposure had been brought about by an incredibly short-sighted blunder on the part of the master mind by which the whole affair had been conceived. William Romayne's was the master mind, and William Romayne, in trying to overreach alike his dupes and his confederates, had overreached himself. His own hand had created the clue which had led eventually to the ruin of the scheme he had originated. His death, with the news of which the London Stock Exchange was ringing only a few hours after it was known in Nice, was the forfeit paid by a strong nature to which success in all its undertakings was the very salt of life.

Mrs. Romayne, on leaving the sitting-room, passed along the passages to her own room—not that which she had entered twenty-four hours before to consult with her husband as to the pleasure expedition of the afternoon—her face and manner altering not at all. Her composure was evidently neither forced nor unreal. The emotion created in her by the tragic circumstances through which she was living was obviously not the heartbroken shame and despair naturally to be attributed to a wife so situated, but a bitter and burning resentment. Had William Romayne passed away in the ordinary course of nature, or by any violent accident, his widow would have mourned him with conventional lamentation and with a certain amount of genuine regret. He had committed suicide, as the letter lying by his side revealed to his wife even while she hardly realised that he was indeed dead, as his only way of escape from the consequences of fraud on the brink of detection; and his widow's attitude to his memory under these circumstances was the natural outcome of the character of their married life.

Hermia Stirling at nineteen had been a pretty, practical, matter-of-fact girl, with her rather shallow nature somewhat prematurely matured. She had been an orphan from her babyhood, and having no near relations in England, her nineteen years of life had been lived under varied auspices, resulting in more desultory education, moral as well as mental, than was good for her. The most impressionable of those years, however—those from fourteen to nineteen—had been passed with connections of her mother's, young and wealthy society women, with no ideas beyond society life, and with little perceptible principle but that of social expediency. Hermia was just nineteen, just out, and taking to the life before her with the ease and zest of a born woman of the world, when one of these ladies died, and the other married and went away to America with her husband. At this juncture the girl's guardian, her father's only brother, returned from India to settle in London with his only child, a girl two years older than Hermia; and it was obvious that his home must be also Hermia's. But neither old Mr. Falconer nor his daughter had the slightest taste or capacity for fashionable life, and before she had spent six months with them the world had become to Hermia an insufferably dull and tiresome place.

She had known William Romayne in society. He was rich, he was handsome, and he was very popular; there was that indefinable something about him, manner, magnetism, or tact, which constitutes a kind of dominating charm. He was not the less "somebody" in that he was vaguely understood to be a business man of some sort, with dealings in shares and stocks all over the world—a locality which lent a picturesque haziness to his affairs. Consequently, when he followed Hermia into her new life and asked her to marry him, she passed over the fact that he was five-and-twenty years her senior, and consented with the practical promptitude of a nature for which romance and sentiment were not. For eighteen months she and her husband had lived in a large house in Eaton Square, entertaining and being entertained through two brilliant seasons, which took away any girlishness which Hermia had ever possessed, and gave her qualities which she admired infinitely more. She found her husband very pleasant, very easy to live with, and, after the first six months, quite unexacting. His business took him into the City every day at this time, though, as his wife said, complacently, he was not the least like the ordinary City man; but at the end of the season which followed on the birth of their child he announced that he would have to spend certainly six months, possibly more, in America.

He showed no ardent desire to take his wife with him, and his wife had no desire whatever to go. She wanted to spend the rest of the summer at one of the fashionable health resorts, and to winter in Rome. Such an arrangement was accordingly made between them in the simplest, most matter-of-fact way, arguing no shadow of ill-will on either side; and during the four years which had elapsed since then, husband and wife had each gone his or her own way, meeting when occasion served for a month or two at a time, now in London, now in Paris, now in Rome; and presumably finding the arrangement mutually satisfactory. The little boy had been left for the most part to the care of Mrs. Romayne's cousin, Frances Falconer. Mrs. Romayne regarded him with the careless, half-dormant affection of a woman to whom her child owes nothing but bare life; to whom its arrival in the world has been rather a tiresome interlude, merely, in her round of pleasures and pursuits; who has had no time since, and has seen no occasion to make time, to give it that care which other people, as it seemed to her, could give it quite as well as she; and who is waiting, vaguely, until it shall be "grown up," to find it interesting.

That her husband's "business" had taken him in the course of those four years into every corner of the globe where the passing of money from hand to hand is elevated into a science, Mrs. Romayne knew; and with that fact her knowledge of his affairs began and ended. He made her an ample allowance; whenever they met she found him the same handsome, rather callous, but withal fascinating man; clever with a cleverness which she could appreciate—the cleverness which made money, and held a position in society—and she had asked nothing more of him. Her regard for him, if regard that could be called which was more truly indifference, had been founded on appreciation of his success. Before failure, before the social disgrace which must be the lot of a detected swindler and suicide, it disappeared totally and instantaneously, to be replaced by a burning sense of personal outrage and insult.

It was late in the afternoon before she left her room again. Dennis Falconer received a message to the effect that Mrs. Romayne was sure that he must be tired, and begged that he would not think of her until he had lunched and rested.

When she did reappear she was in widow's weeds, and the contrast between her dress, with its tragic significance of desolation, and her face, untouched with feeling, was inexpressible.

Dennis Falconer was in the sitting-room when she entered it. His sense of duty was largely developed, and he was also keenly sensible of the moral aspect of the affair with which he was brought into such close contact. The first of these senses kept him in waiting in anticipation of the appearance of the woman for whose assistance he was there; and the second weighed so heavily upon him that the publicity of the hotel smoking-room would have been intolerable to him under the circumstances.

He rose quickly as Mrs. Romayne came in, a look of slight constraint on his face.

Dennis Falconer had no near relation, and perhaps this absence of close ties to England had had something to do with his adoption of the life of a traveller and explorer in connection with the Royal Geographical Society. Old Mr. Falconer, Mrs. Romayne's uncle, was his second cousin only, though the younger man had been brought up to address him as uncle; but in so small a clan distant relationship counts for more than in a family where first cousins and brothers and sisters abound, and there was nothing strange to Dennis Falconer or to Mrs. Romayne in the fact of his coming to her support, even though they hardly knew one another. But Falconer had been chilled and even repelled by her manner of the morning, and he was very conscious now of having his cousin's acquaintance to make, and of approaching the process with a vague prejudice against her in his mind.

This prejudice was not dissipated by her first words, spoken with a suavity somewhat low in pitch, truly, but with a tacit ignoring of the significance of their meeting which seemed to the man she addressed—to whom society life with its obligations and conventionalities was practically an unknown quantity—simply jarring and unsuitable.

"I hope you are rested!" she said. "I suppose, though, that to such a traveller as you are, the journey from London to Nice is nothing. I hear from Frances constantly about your exploits, and she tells me that we are to expect great things of you. What a long time it is since we met!"

She sat down as she spoke, with a hard little smile, and Falconer murmured something almost unintelligible. Thinking that his manner arose from mere embarrassment, instinct dictated to her to set him at his ease; and with no faintest comprehension of his attitude of mind she proceeded to chat to him about his own affairs, asking him questions which elicited coherent answers indeed, but answers which grew terser and sterner until she thought indifferently that her cousin was a rather heavy person. At last there came a pause; a pause during which Falconer gazed grimly and uncomfortably at the floor. And when Mrs. Romayne broke it, it was with a different tone and manner, hard and matter-of-fact.

"The detective told you more than he told me, possibly," she said. "If there is anything more for me to hear, I should like to hear it. You had better, I think, read this letter. Mr. Romayne received it yesterday morning."

She handed him that letter written on blue paper which had lain by the dead man's side, and Falconer took it in silence.

The letter was from one of William Romayne's confederates. It was the desperate letter of a desperate man who knew himself to be addressing the man to whom he was to owe ruin and disgrace. The crisis had evidently been so wholly unexpected that detection was actually imminent before the criminals recognised it as even possible. The gist of the letter was contained in the statement that before it met the eyes of the man for whom it was intended, the whole scheme would be exploded.

Falconer read it through, his face very stern. He finished it and refolded it, still in silence, and Mrs. Romayne said in a dry, thin voice:

"It bears out, as you see, what the detective no doubt told you—that there was so little ground for suspicion three days ago that he was sent out merely to watch, and without even a warrant. He found a telegram waiting for him here from his authorities yesterday morning."

"He told me so!" answered Falconer distantly and constrainedly, handing her back the letter as he spoke without comment.

"There is not the faintest possibility of hushing it up, I conclude?" she asked, in the same hard voice.

Falconer looked at her for a moment, the indefinite disapprobation of her, which had been growing in him almost with every word she said, taking form in his face in a distinct expression of reprobation.

"Not the faintest!" he said emphatically. "Nor do I see that such a possibility is in any way to be desired."

She glanced at him with a quick movement of her eyebrows. She did not speak, however, and a silence ensued between them; one of those uncomfortable silences eloquent of conscious want of sympathy. It was broken this time by Falconer, who spoke with formal politeness and restraint.

"You will wish to get away from this place as soon as possible, no doubt," he said. "There may be some slight delay before we are put into possession of the papers and other effects at present in the hands of the authorities here. But I will, of course, do all I can to hasten matters."

"Thanks!" she said. "The papers? Oh, you mean Mr. Romayne's papers! Are there any, do you think? A will, I suppose?"

"The will, if there is one, will be so much waste paper, I fear," said Falconer with uncompromising sternness. "There is no chance of any property being saved, even if it was possible to wish for such a thing. But there may be papers, nevertheless; in fact, no doubt there must be; and you will, of course, wish to have them."

"Yes," said Mrs. Romayne thoughtfully; "yes, of course." She paused a moment, and then added in a dry, constrained voice: "Do you mean me to understand that I am absolutely penniless?"

"Was your own money in your own hands, or in Mr. Romayne's?"

"In Mr. Romayne's."

"Then I fear there can be no doubt that such is the case."

Falconer spoke very stiffly and distantly, and Mrs. Romayne rose from her chair a little abruptly, and walked to the window. When she turned to him again it was to speak of the formalities necessary with the Nice authorities, and a few moments later the interview was ended by the appearance of dinner.

During the few days that followed, the distance between them, which that first interview established so imperceptibly but so certainly, never lessened; it grew, indeed, with their contact with one another.

To Falconer Mrs. Romayne's whole attitude of mind, her whole personality, was simply and entirely antipathetic. That a woman under such circumstances should speak, and act, and think as Mrs. Romayne spoke, and acted, and—as far as he could tell—thought; with so little sense of any but the social aspect of her husband's crime; with so little realisation of the ruin that crime had brought to hundreds of innocent people; with so little moral feeling of any kind; was in the highest degree reprehensible to him. Having assumed a mental attitude of reprehension, he stopped short; his perceptions were not sufficiently keen to allow of his understanding that some pity might be due also.

Suffering is not always to be estimated by the worth of the object through which it is inflicted; not often, indeed, in this world, where the sum of man's suffering is out of all proportion greater than the sum of man's spirituality. Mrs. Romayne's conception of life might be in the last degree narrow and selfish, and as such it might be in the highest degree to be deprecated; but such as it was it was all she had, and within its limits her life was now in ruin. Her aims and ends in life might be of the poorest, and deserving of unsparing condemnation; but she had nothing beyond, and the pain of their overthrow was to her dormant sensibility not so very disproportionate to the suffering inflicted on a more sensitive organisation by the shattering of higher hopes.

Mrs. Romayne, for her part, found her cousin, with the reserve and formality of demeanour which the situation developed in him, simply a tiresome and uncongenial companion. He was very attentive to her. His manner, as she acknowledged to herself more than once with a heavy sigh, was excellent, and he managed her difficult and painful affairs with admirable strength and tact; she learnt in the course of those few days to respect him and depend on him, in spite of herself and even against her will. But it was not surprising that the end of their enforced dual solitude should be looked for more or less eagerly by both parties. They were almost entirely dependent on one another for companionship. Falconer, it is true, saw Dr. Aston once or twice; but of

Mrs. Romayne's acquaintances not one had even left a card of condolence upon her. Neither the Cloughtons nor any other of the pleasure-seekers who had previously been so anxious for her society, showed any sign of being aware of her existence under her present circumstances.

The form taken by Falconer's first allusion to the probable limits of their detention in Nice had created in both of them, by one of those vague chains of idea which are so unaccountable and so often experienced, a tendency to think and speak of the termination of that detention, when they did speak together on the subject, as "when the papers are given up." There was some question, at one time, as to whether or no even the private papers of William Romayne would be returned to his widow. And these same papers, thus surrounded by an element of painful uncertainty, and at the same time elevated into a kind of order of release, obtained in the minds of both a fictitious importance on their own account. Mrs. Romayne found herself thinking about them, conjecturing about them, even dreaming about them; until at last, when they were actually placed in her hand, they possessed a curious fascination for her.

It was about midday when she and Falconer returned from their final appearance before the authorities. She stood in the middle of the room holding the large, shabby despatch-box, lately handed to her with a grave "Private papers, madame"; the noise of the carnival floated in at the window in striking contrast with the two sombre figures.

"I think I will go and look them over!" she said in a low, rather surprised voice. "You would like to go out, perhaps. Please don't think about me. I will spend the day quietly indoors."

He answered her courteously, and she left the room slowly, with her eyes fixed curiously on the despatch-box in her hand.

CHAPTER IV

MRS. ROMAYNE carried the despatch-box to her bedroom and set it down on a small table. She and Falconer were leaving Nice on the following morning, and her maid was just finishing her packing. Mrs. Romayne inspected the woman's arrangements, gave her sundry orders, and then dismissed her. Left alone, she made one or two trifling preparations for the journey on her own account, and when these were completed to her satisfaction, she drew the table on which she had placed the despatch-box to the open window, and seated herself.

She drew the box towards her and unlocked it, and there was nothing in her face as she did so but the hard resentment which had grown upon it during the last few days, just touched by an indefinite and equally hard curiosity. The interest which those papers possessed for her had been created by purely artificial means; intrinsically they were nothing to her. The position which the possession of them had occupied in her thoughts lately was the sole source of the impulse under which she was acting now; under any other circumstances she might hardly have cared to look at them.

She raised the lid and paused a moment, looking down at the compact mass of papers within with a sudden vague touch of more personal interest. The box was nearly full. The various sets of papers were carefully and methodically fastened together, and endorsed evidently upon a system. Mrs. Romayne hesitated a moment, and then took out a packet at random.

It consisted of bills all bearing dates within the last six months; all sent in by leading London tradesmen, and all for large amounts. Mrs. Romayne glanced at the figures, and her eyebrows moved with an expression of slight surprise, which was almost immediately dominated by bitter acceptance and comprehension. She opened none, however, until she came to one bearing the name of a well-known London jeweller. She read the name and the amount of the bill, and paused; then a new curiosity came into her eyes, and she unfolded the paper quickly. The account was a very long one, and as her eyes travelled quickly down it, taking in item after item, a dull red colour crept into her face, and her eyes sparkled with contemptuous resentment. She was evidently surprised, and yet half-annoyed with herself for being surprised. Two-thirds of the items in the bill in her hand were for articles of jewellery not worn by men, and not one of these had ever been seen by William Romayne's wife.

She stuffed the paper back into its fastening, tossed the bundle away and took another packet from the box with quickened interest. It consisted of miscellaneous documents, all, likewise, connected with her husband's life in London during the past winter, but of no particular interest. The next packet she opened was of the same nature, and with that the top layer of the box came to an end.

The papers below were evidently older; of varying ages, indeed, to judge from their varying tints of yellow. Disarranging a lower layer in taking out the packet nearest to her hand, Mrs. Romayne saw that there were older papers still, beneath, and realised that the box before her contained the private papers of many years; probably all the private papers which William Romayne had preserved throughout his life. She opened the packet she had drawn out, hastily and with an angry glitter in her eyes. It consisted of businesslike-looking documents, not likely, as it seemed, to be of any interest to her.

She glanced through the first unheedingly enough, and then, as she reached the end, something seemed suddenly to touch her attention. She paused a moment, with a startled, incredulous expression on her face, and began to re-read it slowly and carefully. She read it to the end again, and her face, as she finished, was a little pale and chilled-looking. She freed another paper from the packet almost mechanically, with an absorbed, preoccupied look in her eyes, opened it and read it with a strained, hardly comprehending attention which grew gradually and imperceptibly, as she went on from paper to paper, into a kind of stupefied horror. She finished the thick packet in her hands, and then she paused, lifting her pale face for a moment and gazing straight before her with an indescribable expression on its shallow hardness, as though she was realising something almost incredibly bitter and repugnant to her, and was stunned by the realisation. Then her instincts and habits of life and thought seemed to assert themselves, as it were, and to dominate the situation. Her expression changed; the stupefied look gave place to what was little deeper than bitter excitement; a patch of angry colour succeeded the pallor of a moment earlier; and her eyes glittered.

Turning to the despatch-box again, she proceeded to ransack it with a hasty eagerness of touch which differed markedly from the careless composure of her earlier proceedings. Paper after paper was torn open, glanced through—sometimes even re-read with a feverish attention—and tossed aside; sometimes with a sudden deepening of that angry flush; sometimes with a movement of the lips, as though an interjection formed itself upon them; always with a heightening of her excitement; until one packet only remained at the bottom of the box. Mrs. Romayne snatched it out, and then started slightly as she saw that it did not consist, as the majority of the others had done, of business papers, but of letters in a woman's handwriting. Nor was it so old as many of the papers she had looked at, some of which had borne dates twenty-five years back. She opened it with a sudden hardening of her excitement, which seemed to mark the change from almost impersonal to intensely personal interest. She saw that the date was that of the second year after her marriage; that each letter was annotated in her husband's writing;

and then she began deliberately to read, her lips very thin and set, her eyes cold and hard. She read the letters all through, with every comment inscribed on them, and by the time she laid the last upon the table her very lips were white with vindictive feeling strangely incongruous on her little conventional face. She sat quite still for a moment, and then rose abruptly and stood by the window with her back to the table, looking out upon the evening sky.

The strength of feeling died out of her face, however, in the course of a very few minutes, leaving it only very white and rather strange-looking, as though she had received a series of shocks which had made a mark even on material so difficult to impress as her artificial personality; and she turned, by-and-by, and contemplated the table, littered now with documents of all sorts, as though she saw, not the actual heaps of papers, but something beyond them contemptible and disgusting to her beyond expression. Then suddenly she moved forward, crammed the papers indiscriminately into the despatch-box, forced down the lid, and carried the box out of the room down the stairs towards the sitting-room where she had left Dennis Falconer.

It was an impulse not wholly consistent with the self-reliance of her ordinary manner; but that manner had been acquired in a world where shocks and difficulties were more or less disbelieved in. Face to face with so unconventional a condition of affairs Mrs. Romayne's conventional instincts were necessarily at fault; and there being no strong motive power in her to supply their place, it was only natural that she should relieve herself by turning to the man on whom the past few days had taught her to rely.

Dennis Falconer was not in the sitting-room when she opened the door, but as she stood in the doorway contemplating the empty room, he came down the corridor behind her.

"Were you looking for me?" he said with distant courtesy as he reached her. He made a movement to relieve her of the box she carried, and as he did so he was struck by her expression. "Is there anything here you wish me to see?" he said quickly and gravely.

"Yes," she said; she spoke in a dry, hard voice, about which there was a ring of excitement which made him look at her again, and realise vaguely that something was wrong.

He followed her into the room, and she motioned to him to put the box on the table.

"I have been looking them over," she said, indicating the papers with a gesture, "and I have brought them to you. They are very interesting."

She laughed a bitter, crackling little laugh, and the disapproval in ambush in Dennis Falconer's expression developed a little.

"Do you wish me to go over them now, and with you?" he enquired stiffly.

"Not with me, I think, thank you," she answered, the novel excitement about her manner finding expression once more in that harsh laugh. "One reading is enough. But now, if you don't mind. There are business points on which I may possibly be mistaken"—she did not look as though she spoke from conviction—"and—I should like you to read them. I will go out into the garden; it is quite empty always at this time, and I want some air."

Her tone and the glance she cast at the despatch-box as she spoke made it evident that it was not closeness of material atmosphere alone that had created the necessity.

"I will read them now, certainly, if you wish it," he returned.

Then, as she took up a book which lay on a table with a mechanical gesture of acknowledgement, he opened the door for her and she went out of the room. He came back to the table, drew up a chair, and opened the despatch-box.

Two hours later Dennis Falconer was still sitting in that same chair, his right hand, which rested on the table, clenched until the knuckles were white, his face pale to the very lips beneath its tan. In his eyes, fixed in a kind of dreadful fascination on the innocent-looking piles of papers before him, there was a look of shocked, almost incredulous horror, which seemed to touch all that was narrow and dogmatic about his ordinary expression into something deep and almost solemn. The door opened, and he started painfully. It was only the waiter with preliminary preparations for dinner, and recovering himself with an effort Falconer rose, and slowly, almost as though their very touch was repugnant to him, began to replace the papers in the box. He locked it, and then left the room, carrying it with him.

Dinner was served, and Mrs. Romayne had been waiting some two or three minutes before he reappeared. He was still pale, and the horror had rather settled down on to his face than left it; but it had changed its character somewhat; the breadth was gone from it. It was as though he had passed through a moment of expansion and insight to contract again to his ordinary limits. Mrs. Romayne was standing near the window; the excitement had almost entirely subsided from her manner, leaving her only harder and more bitter in expression than she had been three hours before. She glanced sharply at Falconer as he came towards her with a constrained, conventional word or two of apology; answered him with the words his speech demanded; and they sat down to dinner.

It was a silent meal. Mrs. Romayne made two or three remarks on general topics, and asked one or two questions as to their journey of the following day; and Falconer responded as briefly as courtesy allowed. On his own account he originated no observation whatever until dinner was over, and the final disappearance of the waiter had been succeeded by a total silence.

Mrs. Romayne was still sitting opposite him, one elbow resting on the table, her head leaning on her hand as she absently played with some grapes on which her eyes were fixed. Falconer glanced across at her once or twice, evidently with a growing conviction that it was incumbent on him to speak, and with a growing uncertainty as to what he should say. This latter condition of things helped to make his tone even unusually formal and dogmatic as he said at last:

"Sympathy, I fear, must seem almost a farce!"

She glanced up quickly, her eyes very bright and hard.

"Sympathy?" she said drily. "I don't know that there is any new call for sympathy, is there? After all, things are very much where they were!"

A kind of shock passed across Falconer's face; a materialisation of a mental process.

"What we know now——" he began stiffly.

"What we knew before was quite enough!" interrupted Mrs. Romayne. "When one has arrived violently at the foot of the precipice, it is of no particular moment how long one has been living on the precipice's edge. While nothing was known, Mr. Romayne was only on the precipice's edge, and as no one knew of the precipice it was practically as though none existed. Directly one thing came out it was all over! He was over the edge. Nothing could make it either better or worse."

She spoke almost carelessly, though very bitterly, as though she felt her words to be almost truisms, and Falconer stared at her for a moment in silence. Then he said with stern formality, as though he were making a deliberate effort to realise her point of view:

"You imply that Mr. Romayne's fall—his going over the edge of the precipice, if I may adopt your figure—consisted in the discovery of his misdeeds. Do you mean that you think it would have been better if nothing had ever been known?"

Mrs. Romayne raised her eyebrows.

"Of course!" she said amazedly. Then catching sight of her cousin's face she shrugged her shoulders with a little gesture of deprecating concession. "Oh, of course, I don't mean that Mr. Romayne himself would have been any better if nothing had ever come out," she said impatiently. "The right and wrong and all that kind of thing would have been the same, I suppose. But I don't see how ruin and suicide improve the position."

She rose as she spoke, and Falconer made no answer.

Mrs. Romayne had touched on the great realities of life, the everlasting mystery of the spirit of man with its unfathomable obligations and disabilities; had touched on them carelessly, patronisingly, as "all that kind of thing." She was as absolutely blind to the depth of their significance as is a man without eyesight to the illimitable spaces of the sky above him. To Falconer her tone was simply scandalising. He did not understand her ignorance. He could not touch the pathos of its limitations and the possibilities by which it was surrounded. The grim irony of such a tone as used by the ephemeral of the immutable was beyond his ken.

"I have several things to see to upstairs," Mrs. Romayne went on after a moment's pause. "I shall go up now, and I think, if you will excuse me, I will not come down again. We start so early. Good night!"

"Good night!" he returned stiffly; and with a little superior, contemptuous smile on her face she went away.

CHAPTER V

DENNIS FALCONER had been alone for nearly an hour, when his solitude was broken up by the appearance of a waiter, who presented him with a card, and the information that the gentleman whose name it bore was in the smoking-room. The name was Dr. Aston's, and after a moment's reflection Falconer told the waiter to ask the gentleman to come upstairs. Falconer had spent that last hour in meditation, which had grown steadily deeper and graver. It seemed to have carried him beyond the formal and dogmatic attitude of mind with which he had met Mrs. Romayne, back to the borders of those larger regions he had touched when he sat looking at William Romayne's papers; and there was a warmth and gratitude in his reception of Dr. Aston when that gentleman appeared, that suggested that he was not so completely sufficient for himself as usual.

"The smoking-room is very full, I imagine?" he said, as he welcomed the little doctor. "My cousin has gone to bed, and I thought if you didn't mind coming up, doctor, we should be better off here."

Dr. Aston's answer was characteristically hearty and alert. Knowing it to be Falconer's last night at Nice, he had come round, he said, just for a farewell word, and to arrange, if possible, for a meeting later on under happier circumstances. A quiet chat over a cigar was what he had not hoped for, but the thing of all others he would like. He settled himself with a genial instinct for comfort in the arm-chair Falconer pulled round to the window for him; accepted a cigar and prepared to light it; glancing now and again at the younger man's face with shrewd, kindly eyes, which had already noticed something unusual in its expression.

Dr. Aston and Dennis Falconer had met, some six years before, in Africa, under circumstances which had brought out all that was best in the young man's character; and Dr. Aston had been warmly attracted by him. Being a particularly shrewd student of human nature, he had taken his measure accurately enough, subsequently, and knew as certainly as one man may of another where his weak points lay, and how time was dealing with them. But his kindness for, and interest in, Dennis Falconer had never abated; perhaps because his insight did not, as so much human insight does, stop at the weak points.

Dennis Falconer, for his part, regarded Dr. Aston with an affectionate respect which he gave to hardly any other man on earth.

There was a short silence as the two men lit their cigars, and then Dr. Aston, with another glance at Falconer's face, broke it with a kindly, delicate enquiry after Mrs. Romayne. Falconer answered it almost absently, but with an instinctive stiffening, so to speak, of his face and voice, and there was another pause. The doctor was trying the experiment of waiting for a lead. He was just deciding that he must make another attempt on his own account when Falconer took his cigar from between his lips and said, with his eyes fixed on the evening sky:

"I'm always glad to see you, doctor; but I never was more glad than to-night."

A sound proceeded from the doctor which might have been described as a grunt if it had been less delicately sympathetic, and Falconer continued:

"I've been trying to think out a problem, and it was one too many for me: the origin of evil."

He was thoroughly in earnest, and nothing was further from him than any thought of lightness or flippancy. But there was a calm familiarity and matter-of-course acquaintanceship with his subject about his tone that produced a slight quiver about the corners of the little doctor's mouth. He did not speak, however, and the movement with which he took his cigar from between his lips and turned to Falconer was merely sympathetic and interested.

"Of course, I know it's an unprofitable subject enough," continued Falconer almost apologetically. "We shall never be much the wiser on the subject, struggle as we may. But still, now and then it seems to be forced on one. It has been forced on me to-day."

"Apropos of William Romayne?" suggested Dr. Aston, so delicately that the words seemed rather a sympathetic comment than a question.

"Yes," returned Falconer. "We have been looking through his private papers." He paused a moment, and then continued as if drawn on almost in spite of himself. "You knew him by repute, I dare say, doctor. He had one of those strong personalities which get conveyed even by hearsay. A clever man, striking and dominating, universally liked and deferred to. Yet he must have been as absolutely without principle as this table is without feeling."

He struck the little table between them with his open hand as he spoke; and then, as though the expression of his feelings had begotten, as is often the case, an irresistible desire to relieve himself further, he answered Dr. Aston's interested ejaculation as if it had been the question the doctor was at once too well-bred and too full of tact to put.

"There were no papers connected with this last disgraceful affair, of course; those, as you know, I dare say, were all seized in London. It's the man's past life that these private papers throw light on. Light, did I say? It was a life of systematic, cold-blooded villainy, for which no colours could be dark enough."

He had uttered his last sentence involuntarily, as it seemed, and now he laid down his cigar, and turning to Dr. Aston, began to speak low and quickly.

"They are papers of all kinds," he said. "Letters, business documents, memoranda of every description, and two-thirds of them at least have reference to fraud and wrong of one kind or another. Not one penny that man possessed can have been honestly come by. His business was swindling; every one of his business transactions was founded on fraud. He can have had no faith or honesty of any sort or kind. He was living with another woman before he had been married a year. All that woman's letters—he deceived her abominably, and it's fortunate that she died—are annotated and endorsed like his 'business' memoranda; evidently kept deliberately as so much stored experience for future use!"

Dr. Aston had listened with a keen, alert expression of intent interest. His cigar was forgotten, and he laid it down now as if impatient of any distraction, and leant forward over the table with his shrewd, kindly little eyes fixed eagerly on Falconer. Human nature was a hobby of his.

Falconer's confidence, or more truly perhaps the manner of it, had swept away all conventional barriers, and the elder man asked two or three quick, penetrating questions.

"How far back do these records go?" he asked finally.

"They cover five-and-twenty years, I should say," returned Falconer. "The first note on a successful fraud must have been made when he was about four-and-twenty. Why, even then—when he was a mere boy—he must have been entirely without moral sense!"

"Yes!" said the doctor, with a certain dry briskness of manner which was apt to come to him in moments of excitement. "That is exactly what he was, my boy! It was that, in conjunction with his powerful brain, that made him what you called, just now, dominating. It gave him vantage-ground over his fellow-men. He was as literally without moral sense as a colour-blind man is without a sense of colour, or a homicidal maniac without a sense of the sanctity of human life."

An expression of rather horrified and entirely uncomprehending protest spread itself over Falconer's face.

"Romayne was not mad," he objected, with that incapacity for penetrating beneath the surface which was characteristic of him. "I never even heard that there was madness in the family."

"You would find it if you looked far enough, without a doubt!" answered the doctor decidedly. "This is a most interesting subject, Dennis, and it's one that it's very difficult to look into without upsetting the whole theory of moral responsibility, and doing more harm than enough. I don't say Romayne was mad, as the word is usually understood, but all you tell me confirms a notion I have had about him ever since this affair came out. He was what we call morally insane. I'll tell you what first put the idea into my head. It was the extraordinary obtuseness, the extraordinary want of perception, of that blunder of his that burst up the whole thing. Look at it for yourself. It was a flaw in his comprehension of moral sense only possible in a man who knew of the quality by hearsay alone. He must have been a very remarkable man. I wish I had known him!"

"I have heard the term 'moral insanity,' of course," said Falconer slowly and distastefully, ignoring the doctor's last, purely æsthetic sentence, "but it has always seemed to me, doctor, if you'll pardon my saying so, a very dangerous tampering with things that should be sacred even from science. I cannot believe that any man is actually incapable of knowing right from wrong."

"The difficulty is," said the doctor drily, "that the words right and wrong sometimes convey nothing to him, as the words red and blue convey nothing to a colour-blind man, and the endearments of his wife convey nothing to the lunatic who is convinced that she is trying to poison him." He paused a moment, and then said abruptly: "Are there any children?"

Falconer glanced at him and changed colour slightly.

"Yes," he said slowly. "One boy!"

The keen, shrewd face of the elder man softened suddenly and indescribably under one of those quick sympathetic impulses which were Dr. Aston's great charm.

"Heaven help his mother!" he said gently.

Falconer moved quickly and protestingly, and there was a touch of something like rebuke in his voice as he said:

"Doctor, you don't mean to say that you think———"

"You believe in heredity, I suppose?" interrupted the doctor quickly. "Well, at least, you believe in the heredity you can't deny—that a child may—or rather must—inherit, not only physical traits and infirmities, but mental tendencies; likes, dislikes, aptitudes, incapacities, or what not. Be consistent, man, and acknowledge the sequel, though it's pleasanter to shut one's eyes to it, I admit. Put the theory of moral insanity out of the question for the moment if you like; say that Romayne was a pronounced specimen of the common criminal. Why should not his child inherit his father's tendency to crime, his father's aptitude for lying and thieving, as he might inherit his father's eyes, or his father's liking for music—if he had had a turn that way? You're a religious man, Falconer, I know. You believe, I take it, that the sins of the fathers shall be visited on the children. How can they be visited more heavily than in their reproduction? You mark my words, my boy, that little child of Romayne's—unless he inherits strong counter influences from his mother, or some far-away ancestor—will go the way his father has gone, and may end as his father has ended!"

There was a slight sound by the door behind the two men as Dr. Aston finished—finished with a force and solemnity that carried a painful thrill of conviction even through the not very penetrable outer crust of dogma which enwrapped Dennis Falconer—and the latter turned his head involuntarily. The next instant both men had sprung to their feet, and were standing dumb and aghast face to face with Mrs. Romayne. She was standing with her hand still on the lock of the door as if her attention had been arrested just as she was entering the room; she had apparently recoiled, for she was pressed now tightly against the door; her face was white to the very lips, and a vague thought passed through Falconer that he had never seen it before. It was as though the look in her eyes, as she gazed at Dr. Aston, had changed it beyond recognition.

There was a moment's dead silence; a moment during which Dr. Aston turned from red to white and from white to red again, and struggled vainly to find words; a moment during which Falconer could only stare blankly at that unfamiliar woman's face. Then, while the two men were still utterly at a loss, Mrs. Romayne seemed gradually to command herself, as if with a tremendous effort. Gradually, as he looked at her, Falconer saw the face with which he was familiar shape itself, so to speak, upon that other face he did not know. He saw her eyes change and harden as if with the effort necessitated by her conventional instinct against a scene. He saw the quivering horror of her mouth alter and subside in the hard society smile he knew well, only rather stiffer than usual as her face was whiter; and then he heard her speak.

With a little movement of her head in civil recognition of Dr. Aston's presence, she said to Falconer:

"My book is on that table. Will you give it to me, please?"

Her voice was quite steady, though thin. Almost mechanically Falconer handed her the book she asked for, and with another slight inclination of her head, before Dr. Aston had recovered his balance sufficiently to speak, she was gone.

The door closed behind her, and a low ejaculation broke from the doctor. Then he drew a long breath, and said slowly:

"That's a remarkable woman."

Falconer drew his hand across his forehead as though he were a little dazed.

"I think not!" he said stupidly. "Not when you know her!"

"Ah!" returned the doctor, with a shrewd glance at him. "And you do know her?"

If Falconer could have seen Mrs. Romayne an hour later, he would have been more than ever convinced of the correctness of his judgement. The preparations for departure were nearly concluded; she had dismissed her maid and was finishing them herself with her usual quiet deliberation, though her face was very pale and set.

But it might have perplexed him somewhat if he had seen her, when everything was done, stop short in the middle of the room and lift her hands to her head as though something oppressed her almost more heavily than she could bear.

"End as his father ended!" she said below her breath. "Ruin and disgrace!"

She turned and crossed the room to where her travelling-bag stood, and drew from it a letter, thrust into a pocket with several others.

It was the blotted little letter which began "My dear Mamma," and when she returned it to the bag at last, her face was once again the face that Dennis Falconer did not know.

CHAPTER VI

THERE are two diametrically opposed points of view from which London life is regarded by those who know of it only by hearsay; that from which life in the metropolis is contemplated with somewhat awestruck and dubious eyes as necessarily involving a continuous vortex of society and dissipation; and that which recognises no so-called "society life" except during the eight or ten weeks of high pressure known as the season. Both these points of view are essentially false. In no place is it possible to lead a more completely hermit-like life than in London; in no place is it possible to lead a simpler and more hard-working life. On the other hand, that feverish access of stir and movement which makes the months of May and June stand out and focus, so to speak, the attention of onlookers, is only an acceleration and accentuation of the life which is lived in certain strata of the London world for eight or nine months in the year. A large proportion of the intellectual work of the world is done in London; to be in society is a great assistance to the intellectual worker of to-day on his road to material prosperity; consequently a large section of "society" is of necessity in London from October to July; and, since people must have some occupation, even out of the season, social life, in a somewhat lower key, indeed, than the pitch of the season, but on the same artificial foundations, goes on undisturbed, gathering about it, as any institution will do, a crowd of that unattached host of idlers, male and female, whose movements are dictated solely by their own pleasure—or their own weariness.

It was the March of one of the last of the eighties. A wild March wind was taking the most radical liberties with the aristocratic neighbourhood of Grosvenor Place, racing and tearing and shrieking down the chimneys with a total absence of the respect due to wealth. If it could have got in at one in particular of the many drawing-room windows at which it rushed so vigorously, it might have swept round the room and out again with a whoop of amusement. For the room contained some twelve ladies of varying ages and demeanours, and, with perhaps one or two exceptions, each lady was talking at the top of her speed—which, in some cases, was very considerable—and of her voice—which as a rule was penetrating. Every speaker was apparently addressing the same elderly and placid lady, who sat comfortably back in an arm-chair, and made no attempt to listen to any one. Perhaps she recognised the futility of such a course.

The elderly and placid lady was the mistress of the very handsomely and fashionably furnished drawing-room and of the house to which it belonged. Her dress bore traces—so near to vanishing point that their actual presence had something a little ludicrous about it—of the last lingering stage of widow's mourning. Her name was Pomeroy, Mrs. Robert Pomeroy, and she was presiding over the ladies' committee for a charity bazaar.

Fashionable charities and their frequent concomitant, the fashionable bazaars which have superseded the fashionable private theatricals of some years ago, are generally and perhaps uncharitably supposed by a certain class of cynical unfashionables to have their motive power in a feminine love of excitement and desire for conspicuousness. Perhaps there is another aspect under which they may present themselves; namely, as a proof that not even a long course of society life can destroy the heaven-sent instinct for work, even though the circumstances under which it struggles may render it so mere a travesty of the real thing. From this point of view, and when the promoter of a charitable folly is a middle-aged woman, who puts into the business an almost painfully earnest enthusiasm which might have been so useful if she had only known more of any life outside her own narrow round, the situation is not without its pathos. But when, as in the present instance, a long-established, self-reliant, and venerable philanthropic institution is suddenly "discovered," taken up, and patronised by such a woman as the secretary and treasurer of the present committee; a woman who would have been empty-headed and vociferous in any sphere, and who had been moulded by circumstances into a pronounced specimen of a certain type of fashionable woman, dashing, loud, essentially unsympathetic; the position, in the incongruities and discrepancies involved, becomes wholly humorous.

Mrs. Ralph Halse, in virtue of her office as secretary and treasurer, was sitting at Mrs. Pomeroy's right hand; her conception as to the duties of her office seemed to be limited to a sense that it behoved her never for a single instant to leave off addressing the chair, and this duty she fulfilled with a conscientious energy worthy of the highest praise. She had "discovered" the well-known and well-to-do institution before alluded to about a month earlier.

"Such a capital time of year, you know, when one has nothing to do and can attend to things thoroughly!" she had explained to her friends. She had determined that "something must be done," as she had rather vaguely phrased it, and she had applied herself exuberantly and forthwith to the organisation of a bazaar. The season was Lent; philanthropy was the fashion; Mrs. Halse's scheme became the pet hobby of the moment, and the ladies' committee was selected exclusively from among women well known in society.

The committee was tremendously in earnest; nobody could listen to it and doubt that fact for a moment. At the same time a listener would have found some difficulty in determining what was the particular point which had evoked such enthusiasm, because, as has been said, the members were all talking at once. Their eloquence was checked at last, not, as might have been the case with a cold-blooded male committee, by a few short and pithy words from the gently smiling president, but by the appearance of five o'clock tea. The torrent of declamatory enthusiasm thereupon subsided, quenched in the individual consciousness that took possession of each lady that she was "dying for her tea," and had "really been working like a slave." The committee broke up with charming informality into low-toned duets and trios. Even Mrs. Ralph Halse ceased to address the chair, though she could not cease to express her views on the vital point which had roused the committee to a state bordering on frenzy; she turned to her nearest neighbour. Mrs. Halse was a tall woman, good-looking in a well-developed, highly coloured style, and appearing younger than her thirty-eight years. She was dressed from head to foot in grey, and the delicate sobriety of her attire was oddly out of keeping with her florid personality. As a matter of fact, the hobby which had preceded the present all-absorbing idea of the bazaar in her mind—Mrs. Halse was a woman of hobbies—had been ritualism of an advanced type; perhaps some of the fervour with which her latest interest had been embraced was due to a certain sense of flatness in its predecessor; but be that as it may, her present very fashionable attire represented her idea of Lenten mourning.

"I don't see myself how there can be two opinions on the subject," she said. Mrs. Ralph Halse very seldom did see how there could be two opinions on a subject on which her own views were decided. "Fancy dress is a distinct feature, and of course there must be more effect and more variety when each woman is dressed as suits her best, than when there is any attempt at uniform. You agree with me, Lady Bracondale, I'm sure?"

The woman she addressed was of the pronounced elderly aristocratic type, tall and thin, aquiline-nosed and sallow of complexion. She seemed to be altogether superior to enthusiasm of any kind, and her manner was of that unreal kind of dignity and chilling suavity, in which nothing is genuine but its slight touch of condescension.

"Fancy dress is a pretty sight," she said. "But it is perhaps a drawback that of course all the stall-holders cannot be expected to wear it." The words were spoken with an emphasis which plainly conveyed the speaker's sense that no such abrogation of dignity could by any possibility be expected of herself. "What is your opinion, Mrs. Pomeroy?" Lady Bracondale added, turning to the chairwoman of the committee.

Mrs. Pomeroy's attention was not claimed for the moment otherwise than by her serene enjoyment of her cup of tea, which she was sipping with the air of a woman who has done, and is conscious of having done, a hard afternoon's work. Perhaps it is somewhat fatiguing to be talked to by twelve ladies all at once. Lady Bracondale's question was one which Mrs. Pomeroy rarely answered, however, even in her secret heart, so she only smiled now and shook her head thoughtfully.

"Miscellaneous fancy dress gives so much scope for individual taste, don't you think?" said Mrs. Halse.

"Of course it does, my dear Mrs. Halse. Every one can wear what they like, and that is very nice," answered Mrs. Pomeroy comfortably.

"But, on the other hand, a quiet uniform can be worn by any one," said Lady Bracondale with explanatory condescension.

"By any one, of course. So important," assented the chairwoman with bland cheerfulness. Then, as Mrs. Halse's lips parted to give vent to a flood of eloquence, she continued placidly, in her gentle, contented voice: "Mrs. Romayne is not here yet. I wonder what she will say!"

"I met her at the French Embassy last night," said Mrs. Halse, with a slightly aggressive inflection in her voice, "and she told me she meant to come if she could make time. Apparently she has not been able to!"

"Mrs. Romayne?" repeated Lady Bracondale interrogatively. "I don't think I've met her? Really, one feels quite out of the world."

There was a fine affectation of sincerity about the words which would, however, hardly have deceived the most unsophisticated hearer as to the speaker's position in society, or her own appreciation of it. Lady Bracondale was distinctly a person to be known by anybody wishing to make good a claim to be considered in society, and she was loftily conscious of the fact. She had only just returned to town from Bracondale, where she had been spending the last two months.

"Romayne?" she repeated. "Mrs. Romayne! Ah, yes! To be sure! The name is familiar to me. I thought it was. There was a little woman, years ago, whom we met on the Continent. Her husband—dear me, now, what was it? Ah, yes! Her husband failed or—no, of course! I recollect! He was a swindler of some sort. Of course, one never met her again!"

"This Mrs. Romayne is the same, Ralph says," said Mrs. Halse, sipping her tea. "At least, her husband was William Romayne, who was the moving spirit in a big bank swindle—and a lot of other things, I believe—years ago. She turned up about two months ago, and took a house in Chelsea. Lots of money, apparently. She has a grown-up son—he would be grown-up, of course—who is going to the bar."

"But, dear me!" said Lady Bracondale with freezing stateliness, "does she propose to go into society? It was a most scandalous affair, my dear Mrs.

Pomeroy, as far as I remember. A connection of Lord Bracondale's lost some money, I recollect; and I think the man—Romayne, I mean, of course—poisoned himself or something. We were at Nice when it happened. He committed suicide there, and it was most unpleasant! She can't expect one to know her!"

Eighteen years had passed since the same woman had expressed herself as eager to make the acquaintance of "the man," and the haze which had wrapped itself in her mind about the tragedy which had frustrated her desire in that direction, was not the only outcome for her of the passing of those years. Lady Bracondale had been Lady Cloughton eighteen years ago, the wife of the eldest son of the Earl of Bracondale; poor, and with a somewhat perfunctorily yielded position. She and her husband had been, moreover, a cheery, easy-tempered pair, living chiefly on the Continent, and getting a good deal of pleasure out of life. His father's death had given to Lord Cloughton the family title and the family lands; and with his accession to wealth, importance, and responsibilities, his wife's whole personality had gradually seemed to become transformed. Her satisfaction in her new dignities took the form of living rigidly up to what she considered their obligations. Laxity, frivolity of any kind, seemed to her to abrogate from the importance of her position. She ranged herself on the side of strict decorum and respectability, and became more precise than the precisians. Her husband at the same time developed talents latent in his obscurity, and became a prominent politician; and the ultra-correct and exclusive Lady Bracondale was now in truth a power in society.

Consequently, the tone in which she disposed of the intruder, who had ventured unauthorised to obtain recognition during her absence, was crushing and conclusive. But Mrs. Pomeroy's individuality was of too soft a consistency to allow of her being crushed; and she replied placidly, and with unconscious practicality.

"People do know her, dear Lady Bracondale," she said. "She had some friends among really nice people to begin with, and every one has called on her. I really don't know how it has happened, but it is years and years ago, you know, and she really is a delightful little woman. Quite wrapped up in her boy!"

Almost before the words were well uttered, before Lady Bracondale could translate into speech the aristocratic disapproval written stiffly on her face, the door was flung open, and the footman announced "Mrs. Romayne!"

CHAPTER VII

EIGHTEEN years lay between the events which Lady Bracondale recalled so hazily and the Mrs. Romayne who crossed the threshold of Mrs. Pomeroy's drawing-room as the footman spoke her name. Those eighteen years had changed her at once curiously more and curiously less than the years between six-and-twenty and four-and-forty usually change a woman. She looked at the first glance very little older than she had done eighteen years ago; younger, indeed, than she had looked during those early days of her widowhood. Such changes as time had made in her appearance seemed mainly due to the immense difference in the styles of dress now obtaining. The dainty colouring, the cut of her frock, the pose of her bonnet, the arrangement of her hair, with its fluffy curls, all seemed to accentuate her prettiness and to bring out the youthfulness which a little woman without strongly marked features may keep for so long. The fluffy hair was a red-brown now, instead of a pale yellow, and the change was becoming, although it helped greatly, though very subtly, to alter the character of her face. The outline of her features was perhaps a trifle sharper than it had been, and there were sundry lines about the mouth and eyes when it was in repose. But these were obliterated, as a rule, by a characteristic to which all the minor changes in her seemed to have more or less direct reference; a characteristic which seemed to make the very similarity between the woman of to-day and the woman of eighteen years before, seem unreal; the singular brightness and vivacity of her expression. Her features were animated, eager, almost restless; her gestures and movements were alert and quick; her voice, as she spoke to an acquaintance here and there, as she moved up Mrs. Pomeroy's drawing-room, was brisk and laughing. Her dress and demeanour were the dress and demeanour of the day to the subtlest shade; she had been a typical woman of the world eighteen years before; she was a typical woman of the world now. But in the old days the personality of the woman had been dominated by and merged in the type. Now the type seemed to be penetrated by something from within, which was not to be wholly suppressed.

She came quickly down the long drawing-room, smiling and nodding as she came, and greeted Mrs. Pomeroy with a little exaggerated gesture of despair and apology.

"Have you really finished?" she cried. "Is everything settled? How shocking of me!" Then, as she shook hands with Mrs. Halse, she added, with a sweetness of tone which seemed to cover an underlying tendency which was not sweet: "However, we have such a host in our secretary that really one voice more or less makes very little difference."

"Well, really, I don't know that we have settled anything!" said Mrs. Pomeroy. "We have talked things over, you know. It is such a mistake to be in a hurry! Don't you think so?"

"I've not a doubt of it," was the answer, given with a laugh. "My dear Mrs. Pomeroy, I have been in a hurry for the last six weeks, and it's a frightful state of things. You've had a capital meeting, though. Why, I believe I am actually the only defaulter!"

The hard blue eyes were moving rapidly over the room as Mrs. Romayne spoke; there was an eager comprehensive glance in them as though the survey taken was in some sense a survey of material or—at one instant—of a battle-ground; and it gave a certain unreality to their carelessness.

"The only defaulter. Yes," agreed Mrs. Pomeroy comfortably. "And now, Mrs. Romayne, you must let me introduce you to a new member of our committee; quite an acquisition! Why, where—oh!" and serenely oblivious of the stony stare with which Lady Bracondale, a few paces off, was regarding the opposite wall of the room just over the newcomer's bonnet, Mrs. Pomeroy, with her kind fat hand on Mrs. Romayne's arm, approached the exclusive acquisition. "Let me introduce Mrs. Romayne, dear Lady Bracondale!" she said with unimpaired placidity.

The stony stare was lowered an inch or two until it was about on a level with Mrs. Romayne's eyebrows, and Lady Bracondale bowed icily; but at the same moment Mrs. Romayne held out her hand with a graceful little exclamation of surprise. It was not genuine, though it sounded so; those keen, quick, blue eyes had seen Lady Bracondale and recognised her in the course of their owner's progress up the room, and had observed her withdrawal of herself those two or three paces from Mrs. Pomeroy's vicinity; and it was as they rested for an instant only on her in their subsequent survey of the room that that subtle change suggestive of a sense of coming battle had come to them. They looked full into Lady Bracondale's face now with a smiling ease, which was just touched with a suggestion of pleasure in the meeting.

"I hardly know whether we require an introduction," said Mrs. Romayne; she spoke with cordiality which was just sufficiently careless to be thoroughly "good form." "It is so many years since we met, though, that perhaps our former acquaintanceship must be considered to have died a natural death. I am very pleased that it should have a resurrection!"

She finished with a little light laugh, and Lady Bracondale found, almost to her own surprise, that they were shaking hands. If she had been able to analyse cause and effect—which she was not—she would have known that it was that carelessness in Mrs. Romayne's manner that influenced her. A powerful prompter to a freezing demeanour is withdrawn when the other party is obviously insensible to cold.

"It is really too bad of me to be so late!" continued Mrs. Romayne, proceeding to pass over their past acquaintance as a half forgotten recollection to which they were both indifferent, and taking up matters as they stood with the easy unconcern and casual conversationalism of a society woman. "At least it would be if my time were my own just now. But as a matter of fact my sole *raison d'être* for the moment is the getting ready of our little place for my boy. I ought to have shut myself up with carpenters and upholsterers until it was done! I assure you I can't even dine out without a guilty feeling that I ought to be seeing after something or other connected with chairs and tables!"

She finished with a laugh about which there was a touch of artificiality, as there had been about her tone as she alluded to her "boy." Perhaps the only thoroughly genuine point about her, at that moment, was a certain intent watchfulness, strongly repressed, in the eyes with which she met Lady Bracondale's gorgon-like stare; and something about the spirited pose of her head and the lines of her face, always recalling, vaguely and indefinitely, that idea of single combat. Lady Bracondale, however, was not a judge of artificiality, and Mrs. Romayne's manner, with its perfect assurance and careless assumption of a position and a footing in society, affected her in spite of herself. The stony stare relaxed perceptibly as she said, stiffly enough, but with condescending interest:

"You are expecting your son in town?"

"I am expecting him every day, I am delighted to say!" answered Mrs. Romayne, with a little conventional gush of superficial enthusiasm. "Really, you have no idea how forlorn I am without him! We are quite absurdly devoted to one another, as I often tell him, stupid fellow. But I always think—don't you?—that a man is much better out of the way during the agonies of furnishing, so I insisted on his making a little tour while I plunged into the fray. He was very anxious to help, of course, dear fellow. But I told him frankly that he would be more hindrance than help, and packed him off—and made a great baby of myself when he was gone. Of course I have had to console myself by making our little place as perfect as possible, as a surprise for him! You know how these things grow! One little surprise after another comes into one's head, and one excuses oneself for one's extravagance when it's for one's boy."

"Are you thinking of settling in London?" enquired Lady Bracondale.

She was unbending moment by moment in direct contradiction of her preconceived determination. Mrs. Romayne was so bright and so unconscious. She ran off her pretty maternal platitudes with such careless confidence, that iciness on Lady Bracondale's part would have assumed a futile and even ridiculous appearance.

"Yes!" was the answer. "We are going to settle down a regular cosy couple. It has been our castle in the air all the time his education has been going on. He is to read for the bar, and I tell him that he will value a holiday more in another year or two, poor fellow. But I'm afraid I bore about him frightfully!" she added, with another laugh. "And it is rather hard on him, poor boy, for he really is not a bore! I think you will like him, Lady Bracondale. I remember young men always adored you!"

Lady Bracondale smiled, absolutely smiled, and said graciously—graciously for her, that is to say:

"You must bring him to see me! I should like to call upon you if you will give me your card."

Mrs. Romayne was in the act of complying—complying with smiling indifference, which was the very perfection of society manner—when Mrs. Pomeroy, evidently moved solely by the impetus of the excited group of ladies of which she was the serenely smiling centre, bore cheerfully down upon them.

"Perhaps we ought to vote about the fancy dress before we separate this afternoon," she suggested, "or shall we talk it over a little more at the next meeting? Perhaps that would be wiser. Mrs. Romayne———"

She looked invitingly at Mrs. Romayne as if for her opinion on the subject, and the invitation was responded to with that ever-ready little laugh.

"Oh, let us put it off until the next meeting," she said. "I am ashamed to say that I really must run away now. But at the next meeting I promise faithfully to be here at the beginning and stay until the very end."

Whereupon it became evident that the greater part of the committee was anxious to postpone the decision on the knotty point in question, and was conscious of more or less pressing engagements. A general exodus ensued, Mrs. Halse alone remaining to expound her views to Mrs. Pomeroy all by herself and in a higher and more conclusive tone than before.

A neat little coupé was waiting for Mrs. Romayne. She gave the coachman the order "home" at first, and then paused and told him to go to a famous cigar merchant's. She got into the carriage with a smiling gesture of farewell to Lady Bracondale, whose brougham passed her at the moment; but as she leant back against the cushions the smile died from her lips with singular suddenness. It left her face very intent; the eyes very bright and hard, the lips set and a little compressed. The lines about them and about her eyes showed out faintly under this new aspect of her face in spite of the eager satisfaction which was its dominant expression. The battle had evidently been fought and won and the victor was ready and braced for the next.

She got out at the cigar merchant's, and when she returned to her carriage there was that expression of elation about her which often attends the perpetration of a piece of extravagance. But as she was driven through the fading sunlight of the March afternoon towards Chelsea, her face settled once more into that intent reflection and satisfaction.

It was a narrow slip of a house at which her coupé eventually stopped, wedged in among much more imposing-looking mansions in the most fashionable part of Chelsea. But what it lacked in size it made up in brightness and general smartness. It had evidently been recently done up with all the latest improvements in paint, window-boxes, and fittings generally, and it presented a very attractive appearance indeed.

Mrs. Romayne let herself in with a latch-key, and went quickly across the prettily decorated hall into a room at the back of what was evidently the dining-room. She opened the door, and then stood still upon the threshold.

The light of the setting sun was stealing in at the window, the lower half of which was filled in with Indian blinds; and as it fell in long slanting rays across the silent room, it seemed to emphasize and, at the same time, to soften and beautify an impression of waiting and of expectancy that seemed to emanate from everything that room contained. It was furnished—it was not large—as a compromise between a smoking-room and a study, and its every item, from the bookcases and the writing-table to the bronzes on the mantelpiece, was in the most approved and latest style, and of the very best kind. Every conceivable detail had evidently been thought out and attended to; the room was obviously absolutely complete and perfect—only on the writing-table something seemed lacking, and some brown paper parcels lay there waiting to be unfastened—and it had as obviously never been lived in. It was like a body without a soul.

The lingering light stole along the wall, touching here and there those unused objects waiting, characterless, for that strange character which the personality of a man impresses always on the room in which he lives, and its last touch fell upon the face of the woman standing in the doorway. The artificiality of its expression was standing out in strong relief as if in half conscious, half instinctive struggle with something that lay behind, something which the aspect of that empty room had developed out of its previous intentness and excitement. With a little affected laugh, as though some one else had been present—or as though affectation were indeed second nature to her—Mrs. Romayne went up to the writing-table and began to undo the parcels lying there. They contained a very handsome set of fittings for a man's writing-table, and she arranged them in their places, clearing away the paper with scrupulous care, and with another little laugh.

"What a ridiculous woman!" she said half aloud, with just the intonation she had used in speaking to Lady Bracondale of her "little surprises" for "her boy." "And what a spoilt fellow!"

She turned away, went out of the room, with one backward glance as she closed the door, and upstairs to the drawing-room. She had just entered the room when a thought seemed to strike her.

"How utterly ridiculous!" she said to herself. "I quite forgot to notice whether there were any letters!"

She was just crossing the room to ring for a servant when the front-door bell rang vigorously and she stopped short. With an exclamation of surprise she went to the door and stood there listening, that she might prepare herself beforehand for the possible visitor, for whom she evidently had no desire. "How tiresome!" she said to herself. "Who is it, I wonder?" She heard the parlourmaid go down the hall and open the door.

"Mrs. Romayne at home?"

With a shock and convulsion, which only the wildest leap of the heart can produce, the listening face in the drawing-room doorway, with the conventional smile which might momently be called for just quivering on it, half in abeyance, half in evidence, was suddenly transformed. Every trace of artificiality fell away, blotted out utterly before the swift, involuntary flash of mother love and longing with which those hard blue eyes, those pretty, superficial little features were, in that instant, transfigured. The elaborately dressed figure caught at the door-post, as any homely drudge might have done; the woman of the world, startled out of—or into—herself, forgot the world.

"It's Julian!" the white, trembling lips murmured. "Julian!"

As she spoke the word, up the stairs two steps at a time, there dashed a tall, fair-haired young man who caught her in his arms with a delighted laugh—her own laugh, but with a boyish ring of sincerity in it.

"I've taken you by surprise, mother!" he cried. "You've never opened my telegram!"

CHAPTER VIII

MRS. ROMAYNE had been left, eighteen years before, absolutely penniless. When Dennis Falconer took her back from Nice to her uncle's home in London, she had returned to that house wholly dependent, for herself and for her little five-year-old boy, on the generosity she would meet with there. Fortunately old Mr. Falconer was a rich man. There had been a good deal of money in the Falconer family, and as its representatives decreased in number, that money had collected itself in the hands of a few survivors.

A long nervous illness, slight enough in itself, but begetting considerable restlessness and irritability, had followed on her return to London. So natural, her tender-hearted cousin and uncle had said, though, as a matter of fact, such an illness was anything but natural in such a woman as Mrs. Romayne, and anything but consistent with her demeanour during the early days of her widowhood. Partly by the advice of the doctor, partly by reason of the sense, unexpressed but shared by all concerned, that London was by no means a desirable residence for the widow of William Romayne, old Mr. Falconer and his daughter left their quiet London home and went abroad with her. No definite period was talked of for their return to England, and they settled down in a charming little house near the Lake of Geneva.

In the same house, when Julian was seven years old, Frances Falconer died. Her death was comparatively sudden, and the blow broke her father's heart. From that time forward his only close interests in life were Mrs. Romayne and her boy. The vague expectation of a return to London at some future time faded out altogether. Mr. Falconer's only desire was to please his niece, and she, with the same tendency towards seclusion which had dictated their first choice of a Continental home, suggested a place near Heidelberg. Here they lived for five years more, and then Mr. Falconer, also, died, leaving the bulk of his property to Mrs. Romayne. The remainder was to go to Dennis Falconer; to his only other near relation, William Romayne's little son, he left no money.

So seven years after her husband's death Mrs. Romayne was a rich woman again; rich and independent as she had never been before, and practically alone in the world with her son. In her relations with her son, those seven years had brought about a curious alteration or developement.

The dawnings of this change had been observed by Frances Falconer during the early months of Mrs. Romayne's widowhood. She had spoken to her father with tears in her eyes of her belief that her cousin was turning for consolation to her child. Blindly attached to her cousin, she had never acknowledged her previous easy indifference as a mother. She stood by while the first place in little Julian's easy affections was gradually won away from herself not only without a thought of resentment, but without any capacity for the criticism of Mrs. Romayne's demeanour in her new capacity as a devoted mother. To her that devotion was the natural and beautiful outcome of the overthrow of her cousin's married life. To sundry other people the new departure presented other aspects. Dennis Falconer, spending a few days at the house near the Lake of Geneva, regarded with eyes of stern distaste what seemed to him the most affected, superficial travesty of the maternal sentiment ever exhibited. Meditating upon the subject by himself, he referred Mrs. Romayne's assumption of the character of devoted mother to the innate artificiality of a fashionable woman denied the legitimate outlet of society life. He went away marvelling at the blindness of his uncle and cousin, and asking himself with heavy disapprobation how long the pose would last.

Time, as a matter of fact, seemed only to confirm it. The half-laughing, wholly artificial manner with which Mrs. Romayne had alluded to her "boy" in Mrs. Pomeroy's drawing-room was the same manner with which, in his early school-days, she had alluded to her "little boy," only developed by years. Mr. Falconer's death and her own consequent independence had made no difference in her way of life. Julian's education had been proceeded with on the Continent as had been already arranged, his mother living always near at hand that they might be together whenever it was possible. In his holidays they took little luxurious tours together. But into society Mrs. Romayne went not at all until Julian was over twenty; when the haze of fifteen years had wound itself about the memory of William Romayne and his misdeeds.

Of those misdeeds William Romayne's son knew nothing. The one point of discord between old Mr. Falconer and his niece had been her alleged intention of keeping the truth from him, if possible, for ever. Mr. Falconer's death removed the only creature who had a right to protest against her decision. When Julian, as he grew older, asked his first questions about his father, she told him that he had "failed," and had died suddenly, and begged him not to question her. And the boy, careless and easy-going, had taken her at her word.

With the termination of Julian's university career, it became necessary that some arrangement should be made for his future. As Julian grew up, the topic had come up between the mother and son with increasing frequency, introduced as a rule not, as might have been expected, by the young man, whom it most concerned, but by Mrs. Romayne. From the very first it had been presented to him as a foregone conclusion that the start in life to which he was to look forward was to be made in London. London was to be their home, and he was to read for the English bar; on these premises all Mrs. Romayne's plans and suggestions were grounded, and Julian's was not the nature to carve out the idea of a future for himself in opposition to that presented to him. Consequently the arrangements, of which the bright little house in Chelsea was the preliminary outcome, were matured with much gaiety and enthusiasm, in what Mrs. Romayne called merrily "a family council of two"; and a certain touch of feverish excitement which had pervaded his mother's consideration of the subject, moved Julian to a carelessly affectionate compunction in that it was presumably for his sake that she had remained so long away from the life she apparently preferred.

The arrangement by which Mrs. Romayne eventually came to London alone was not part of the original scheme. As the time fixed for their departure thither drew nearer, that feverish excitement increased upon her strangely. It seemed as an expression of the nervous restlessness that possessed her that she finally insisted on his joining some friends who were going for two months to Egypt, and leaving her to "struggle with the agonies of furnishing," as she said, alone.

The arrangement had separated the mother and son for the first time within Julian's memory. The fact had, perhaps, had little practical influence on his enjoyment in the interval, but it gave an added fervour to his boyish demonstration of delight in that first moment of meeting as he held her in his vigorous young arms, and kissed her again and again.

"To think of my having surprised you, after all!" he cried gleefully, at last. "You ought to have had my telegram this morning. Why, you've got nervous while you've been alone, mother! You're quite trembling!"

Mrs. Romayne laughed a rather uncertain little laugh. She was indeed trembling from head to foot. Her face was very pale still, but as she raised it to her son the strange, transfigured look had passed from it utterly, and her normal expression had returned to it in all its superficial liveliness, brought back by an effort of will, conscious or instinctive, which was perceptible in the slight stiffness of all the lines. At the same moment she seemed to become aware of the close, clinging pressure with which her hand had closed upon the arm which held her, and she relaxed it in a gesture of playful rebuke and deprecation.

"What would you have, bad boy?" she said lightly. "Don't you know I hate surprises? Oh, I suppose you want to flatter yourself that your poor little mother can't get on without you to take care of her! Well, perhaps she can't, very well. There's a demoralising confession for you, sir!"

But it was not such a confession as her face had been only a few minutes before; in fact, the spoken words seemed rather to belie that mute witness. They were spoken in her ordinary tone, and the gesture with which she laid her hand on his arm to draw him into the drawing-room was one of her usual pretty, affected gestures—as sharp a contrast as possible to the first clinging, unconscious touch.

"Let me look at you," she said gaily, "and make sure that I have got my own bad penny back from Africa, and not somebody else's!"

She drew him laughingly into the fullest light the fading day afforded, and proceeded to "inspect" him, as she said, her face full of a superficial vivacity, which seemed to be doing battle all the time with something behind—something which looked out of her hard, bright eyes, eager and insistent.

Julian Romayne was a tall, well-made young man—taller by a head than the mother smiling up at him; he was well developed for his twenty-three years, slight and athletic-looking, and carrying himself more gracefully than most young Englishmen. But except in this particular, and in a slight tendency towards the use of more gesture than is common in England, his foreign training was in no wise perceptible in his appearance. The first impression he made on people who knew them both was that he was exactly like his mother, and that his mother's features touched into manliness were a very desirable inheritance for her son; for he was distinctly good-looking. But as a matter of fact, only the upper part of his face, and his colouring, were Mrs. Romayne's. He had the fair hair which had been hers eighteen years ago; he had her blue eyes and her pale complexion, and his nose and the shape of his brow were hers. But his mouth was larger and rather fuller-lipped than his mother's, and the line of the chin and jaw was totally different. No strongly-marked characteristics, either intellectual or moral, were to be read in his face; his expression was simply bright and good-tempered with the good temper which has never been tried, and is the result rather of circumstances than of principle.

That strange something in Mrs. Romayne's face seemed to retreat into the depths from which it had come as she looked at him. She finished her inspection with a gay tirade against the coat which he was wearing, and Julian replied with a boyish laugh.

"I knew you'd be down upon it!" he said. "I say, does it look so very bad? I'll get a new fit out to-morrow—two or three, in fact! Mother, what an awfully pretty little drawing-room! What an awfully clever little mother you are!"

He flung his arm round her again with the careless, affectionate demonstrativeness which her manner seemed to produce in him, and looked round the room with admiring eyes. They were the eyes of a young man who knew better than some men twice his age how a room should look, and whose appreciation was better worth having than it seemed.

"You're quite ready for me, you see!" he declared delightedly. "What did you mean, I should like to know, by wanting to keep me away for another fortnight?"

There was a moment's pause before Mrs. Romayne spoke. She looked up into his face with a rather strange expression in her eyes, and then looked away across the room to where a little pile of accepted invitations lay on her writing-table. That curious light at once of battle and of triumph was strong upon her face as it had not been yet.

"Yes," she said at last, and there was an unusual ring about her voice. "I am quite ready for you!"

Something more than the furnishing of a house had gone to the preparation of a place in society for the widow and son of William Romayne, and only the woman who had effected that preparation knew how, and how completely it had been achieved.

A moment later Mrs. Romayne's face had changed again, and she was laughing lightly at Julian's comments as she disengaged herself from his hold, and went towards the bell.

"Foolish boy!" she said as she rang. "I'm glad you think it's nice. We'll have some tea."

She had just poured him out a cup of tea, and quick, easy question and answer as to his crossing were passing between them, when the front-door bell rang, and she broke off suddenly in her speech.

"Who can that be?" she said. "Hardly a caller; it must be six o'clock! Now, I wonder whether, if it should be a caller, Dawson will have the sense to say not at home? Perhaps I had better———" she rose as she spoke, and moved quickly across the room to the door. But she was too late! As she opened the drawing-room door she heard the street door open below, and heard the words, "At home, ma'am." With the softest possible ejaculation of annoyance she closed the door stealthily.

"Such a nuisance!" she said rapidly. "What a time to call! I trust they won't———" And thereupon her face changed suddenly and completely into her usual society smile as the door opened again, and she rose to receive her visitors. "My dear Mrs. Halse!" she exclaimed, "why, what a delightful surprise! Now, don't say that you have come to tell me that anything has gone wrong about the bazaar?" she continued agitatedly. "Don't tell me that, Miss Pomeroy!"

She was shaking hands with her younger visitor as she spoke, a girl of apparently about twenty, very correctly dressed, as pretty as a girl can be with neither colour, expression, nor startlingly correct features, whose eyes are for the most part fastened on the ground. She was Mrs. Pomeroy's only child. She did not deal Mrs. Romayne the blow which the latter appeared to anticipate, but reassured her in a neatly constructed sentence uttered in a rather demure but perfectly self-possessed voice.

Mrs. Halse had been prevented for the moment from monopolising the conversation by reason of her keen interest in the good-looking young man standing by the fireplace; but Miss Pomeroy's words were hardly uttered before she turned excitedly to Mrs. Romayne. If she was going to make a mistake the disagreeables of the position would be with her hostess, she had decided.

"It's your son, Mrs. Romayne?" she cried. "It must be, surely! Such a wonderful likeness! Only, really, I can hardly believe that your son—I was ridiculous enough to expect quite a boy! Oh, don't say that he has just arrived and we are interrupting your first *tête-à-tête*! How truly frightful! Let me tell you this moment what I came for and fly!"

Mrs. Romayne answered her with a suave smile.

"I am going to introduce my boy first, if you don't mind," she said, and then as Julian, in obedience to her look, came forward, with the easy alacrity of a young man whose social instincts are of the highly civilised kind, she laid her hand on his arm with an artificial air of affectionate pride, and continued lightly: "Your first London introduction, Julian. Mrs. Ralph Halse, Miss Pomeroy! He has only just arrived, as you guessed," she added in an aside to Mrs. Halse, "and no doubt he is furiously angry with me for allowing him to be caught with the dust of his journey on him."

But Julian's anger was not perceptible in his face, or in his manner, which was very pleasant and ready. Even after he had handed tea and cake and subsided into conversation with Miss Pomeroy, Mrs. Halse found it difficult to concentrate herself on the business which had brought her to Chelsea. Her speech to Mrs. Romayne, as to the brilliant idea which had struck her just after the committee broke up, was as voluble as usual, certainly, but less connected than it might have been.

"That's all right, then. Such a weight off my mind!" she said, as she copied an address into her note-book with a circumstance and importance which would have befitted the settlement of the fate of nations. "It is so important to get things settled at once, don't you think so? The moment it occurred to me I saw how important it was that there should not be a moment's delay, and I said to Maud Pomeroy: 'Let us go at once to Mrs. Romayne, and she will give us the address, and then dear Mrs. Pomeroy can write the letter tonight.'" Here Mrs. Halse's breath gave out for the moment, and she let her eyes, which had strayed constantly in the direction of Julian and Miss Pomeroy, rest on the young man's good-looking, well-bred face. "We must have your son among the stewards, Mrs. Romayne," she said. "So important! Now, I wonder whether it has occurred to you, as it has occurred to me, that a man or two—just a man or two"—with an impressive emphasis on the last word, as though three men would be altogether beside the mark—"would be rather an advantage on the ladies' committee? Now, what is your opinion, Mr. Romayne? Don't you think you could be very useful to us?"

She turned towards Julian as she spoke, quite regardless of the fact that Miss Pomeroy's correctly modulated little voice was stopped by her tones; and Mrs. Romayne turned towards him also. He and Miss Pomeroy were sitting together on the other side of the room, and as her eye fell upon the pair, a curious little flash, as of an idea or a revelation, leaped for an instant into Mrs. Romayne's eye.

Julian moved and transferred his attention to Mrs. Halse, with an easy courtesy which was a curiously natural reproduction of his mother's more artificial manner, and which was at the same time very young and unassuming. He laughed lightly.

"I shall be delighted to be a steward," he said, "or to be useful in any way. But the idea of a ladies' committee is awe-inspiring."

"You would make great fun of us at your horrid clubs, no doubt," retorted Mrs. Halse. "Oh, I know what you young men are! But you can be rather useful in these cases sometimes, though, of course, it doesn't do to tell you so."

She laughed loudly, and then rose with a sudden access of haste.

"We must really go!" she said. "Maud"—Mrs. Halse had innumerable girl friends, all of whom she was wont to address by their Christian names—"Maud, we are behaving abominably. We mustn't stay another moment, not another second."

But they did stay a great many other seconds, while Mrs. Halse pressed Julian into the service of the bazaar in all sorts and kinds of capacities, and managed to find out a great deal about his past life in the process. When at last she swooped down upon Maud Pomeroy, metaphorically speaking, as though that eminently decorous young lady had been responsible for the delay, and carried her off in a very tornado of protestation, attended to the front door, as in courtesy bound, by Julian, Mrs. Romayne, left alone in the drawing-room, let her face relax suddenly from its responsive brightness into an unmistakeable expression of feminine irritation and dislike.

"Horrid woman!" she said to herself. "Patronises me! Well, she will talk about nothing but Julian all this evening, wherever she may be—and she goes everywhere—so perhaps it has been worth while to endure her." Then, as Julian appeared again, she said gaily: "My dear boy, they've been here an hour, and we shall both be late for dinner! Be off with you and dress!"

It was a very cosy little dinner that followed. Mrs. Romayne, as carefully dressed for her son as she could have been for the most critical stranger, was also at her brightest and most responsive. They talked for the most part of people and their doings; society gossip. Mrs. Romayne told Julian all about Mrs. Halse's bazaar; deriding the whole affair as an excuse for deriding its promoter, but with no realisation of its innate absurdity; and giving Julian to understand, at the same time, that it was "the thing" to be in it; an idea which he was evidently quite capable of appreciating. Dinner over, she drew his arm playfully through hers and took him all over the house.

"Let me see that you approve!" she said with a laughing assumption of burlesque suspense.

The last room into which she took him was the little room at the back of the dining-room; and as his previous tone of appreciation and pleasure developed into genuine boyish exclamations of delight at the sight of it, the instant's intense satisfaction in her face struck oddly on her manner.

"You like it, my lord?" she said. "My disgraceful extravagance is rewarded by your gracious approval? Then your ridiculous mother is silly enough to be pleased." She gave him a little careless touch, half shake and half caress, and Julian threw his arm round her rapturously.

"I should think I did like it!" he said boyishly. "I say, shan't I have to work hard here! Mother, what an awfully jolly smoking table!"

"Suppose you smoke here now," suggested Mrs. Romayne, "by way of taking possession? Oh, yes! I'll stay with you."

She sat down, as she spoke, in one of the low basket-chairs by the fire, taking a little hand-screen from the mantelpiece as she did so. And Julian, with an exclamation of supreme satisfaction, threw himself into a long lounging-chair with an air of general proprietorship which sat oddly on his youthful figure; and proceeded to select and light a cigar.

A silence followed—rather a long silence. Julian lay back in his chair, and smoked in luxurious contentment. Mrs. Romayne sat with her dainty head, with its elaborate arrangement of red-brown hair, resting against a cushion, her face half hidden by the shade thrown by the fire-screen as she held it up in one slender, ringed hand. She seemed to be looking straight into the fire; as a matter of fact her eyes were fixed on the boyish face beside her. She was the first to break silence.

"It is two, nearly three, months since we were together," she said.

The words might have been the merest comment in themselves; but there was something in the bright tone in which they were spoken, something— half suggestion, half invitation—which implied a desire to make them the opening of a conversation. Julian Romayne's perceptions, however, were by no means of the acutest, and he detected no undertone.

"So it is!" he assented, with dreamy cheerfulness.

"How long did you spend in Cairo?"

The question, which came after a pause, was evidently another attempt on a new line. Again it failed.

"Didn't I tell you? Ten days!" said Julian lazily.

Mrs. Romayne changed her position. She leant forward, her elbow on her knee, her cheek resting on her hand, the screen still shading her face.

"The catechism is going to begin," she said gaily.

Julian's cigar was finished. He roused himself, and dropped the end into the ash-tray by his side as he said with a smile:

"What catechism?"

"Your catechism, sir," returned his mother. "Do you suppose I am going to let you off without insisting on a full and particular account of all your doings during the last ten weeks?"

"A full and particular account of all my doings!" he said. "I say, that sounds formidable, doesn't it? The only thing is, you've had it in my letters."

"The fullest and most particular?" she laughed.

"The fullest and most particular!"

"Never mind," she exclaimed, leaning back in her chair again with a restless movement, "I shall catechise all the same. My curiosity knows no limits, you see. Now, you are on your honour as a—as a spoilt boy, understand."

"On my honour as a spoilt boy! All right. Fire away, mum!"

He pulled himself up, folding his hands with an assumption of "good little boy" demeanour, and laughing into her face. She also drew herself up, and laughed back at him.

"Question one: Have you lost your heart to any pretty girl in the past ten weeks?"

"No, mum."

"Question two: Have you flirted—much—with any girl, pretty or plain?"

"No, mum."

"Have you overdrawn your allowance?"

"No, mum. I've got such a jolly generous mother, mum!"

"Have you—— Oh! Have you any secrets from your mother?"

The question broke from her in a kind of cry, but she turned it before it was finished into burlesque, and Julian burst into a shout of laughter.

"Not a solitary secret! There, will that do?"

She was looking straight into his face—her own still in shadow—and there was a moment's pause; almost a breathless pause on her part it seemed; then she broke into a laugh.

"That will do capitally," she said. "The catechism is over."

She rose as she spoke, and added a word or two about a note she had to write.

"We may as well go up into the drawing-room if you have finished smoking," she said. "It is an invitation from some friends of the Pomeroys—a dinner. By-the-bye, don't you think Miss Pomeroy a very pretty girl?"

Julian's response was rather languid, but his mother did not press the point. She turned away to replace the screen on the mantelpiece, and as she did so a thought seemed to strike her.

"Oh, Julian!" she said. "Did you go to Alexandria? What about those curtains you were to get me?"

Her back was towards Julian, and she did not notice the instant's hesitation which preceded his reply. He was putting his cigar-case into his pocket, and the process seemed to demand all his attention.

"I didn't go to Alexandria, unfortunately," he said lightly. "The Fosters had been there, and didn't care to go again."

The clock struck twelve that night when Mrs. Romayne rose at last from the chair in front of her bedroom fireplace in which she had been sitting for more than an hour. The fire had gone out before her eyes unnoticed, and she shivered a little as she rose. Her face was strangely pale and haggard-looking, and the red-brown hair harmonised ill with the anxiety of its look.

"It begins from to-night!" she said to herself. "It is his man's life that begins from to-night!"

CHAPTER IX

"QUITE a presentable fellow!"

There was an unusual ring of excitement in Mrs. Romayne's voice; it was about ten o'clock in the evening, and she was standing in the middle of her own drawing-room, looking up into Julian's face, as he stood before her, having just come into the room, smiling back at her with a certain touch of excitement about his appearance also. He was in evening dress; he had evidently bestowed particular pains upon his attire, and the flower in his buttonhole was an exceptionally dainty one.

Mrs. Romayne was also in evening dress, and in evening dress of the most elaborate description. From the point of view of the fashion of the day, her appearance was absolutely perfect; no detail, from the arrangement of her hair to the point of the silk shoe just visible beneath her skirt, had been neglected; everything was in good taste and in the height of fashion, and the effect of the whole, heightened by the background afforded by the quiet little drawing-room with its softly shaded lamps, was almost startling in its suggestion of luxury and refinement. The fashion of the moment was peculiarly becoming to Mrs. Romayne, and evening dress, with its artificialities and its conventionalities, always enhanced her good points, strictly conventional as they were. With that light of excitement on her face, and a certain suggestion about her of verve and vivacity, she looked almost charming enough to justify the boyish exclamations of exaggerated admiration into which Julian had broken on entering the room.

There was an eager, restless happiness in her eyes, which leapt up into almost triumphant life as she gave a little touch to Julian's buttonhole; and then pushed him a step or two further back, that she might look at him again, and repeated her commendatory words with a laugh. Then, on a little gesture from her, he picked up her cloak, which lay on a chair near, put it carefully about her, and, opening the door for her, followed her downstairs.

Nearly three weeks had elapsed since Julian's arrival in London, and in that time, short as it was, his expression had changed somewhat. There was a quickened interest and alertness about it which detracted from his boyishness, inasmuch as it made him look as though life had actually begun for him. It would have been wholly untrue to say that any touch of responsibility or ambition had dawned upon his good-looking young face; but a subtle something had come to it which was, perhaps, a materialisation of a mental movement which did duty for those emotions. In the course of those three weeks he had had several interviews with the man with whom he was to read; all the preliminaries of his legal career had been settled; and in more than one half-laughing talk with his mother on the conclusion of some arrangement, the preliminaries had been far outstripped, and he had been conducted in triumph to the bench itself.

But in all these buildings of castles in the air, there was a factor in the foundations of his fortunes never allowed by his mother to drop out of sight; the main factor it became when she was the architect, relegating to a subordinate position even the hard work on which Julian was wont to expatiate with enthusiasm and energy. Sometimes as a means, sometimes as an end, sometimes as the sum total of all human ambition, social success, social position were woven into all his schemes for the future as they talked together; woven in with no direct statements or precepts; but with an insidious insistence, and a tacit assumption of their value in the scale of things as a truism in no need of formulation.

Society life had begun for him with the very day after his arrival in town, and had moved briskly with him through the following weeks; briskly, but in a small way. Easter had intervened, and no large entertainments had been given. To-night was to be, as Mrs. Romayne said gaily as she settled her train and her cloak in the brougham into which he had followed her, his first public appearance. They were on their way to the first "smart affair" of the coming season; a dance to be given at a house in Park Lane; not very large, but very desirable, at which—again on Mrs. Romayne's authority—all the right people would be.

"You must dance, of course, but not all the evening, Julian!" his mother said, as their drive drew to an end. "I shall want to introduce you a good deal. And don't engage yourself for supper if you can help it. I'm sorry to be so hard upon you!"

She finished with a laugh, light as her tone had been throughout. Then their carriage drew up suddenly, and her face, in shadow for the moment, changed strangely. For an instant all the happiness, all the excitement and superficiality died out of it, quenched in a kind of revelation of heartsick anxiety so utterly out of all proportion with the occasion, as to be absolutely ghastly; ghastly as only a momentary revelation of the cruel cross-purposes and incongruities of life can be. The next moment, as Julian sprang out of the carriage and turned to help her out, her expression changed again.

It took them some time to get up to the drawing-room, for though the party was by no means a crush, they had arrived at the most fashionable moment, and the staircase was crowded. Salutations, conveyed by graceful movements of the head, passed across an intervening barrier of gay dresses and black coats between Mrs. Romayne and numbers of acquaintances above her or below her on the stairs; and as she smiled and bowed she murmured comments to Julian—names or data, criticisms of dress or appearance—until at last patience, and the continual movement of the stream of which they made part, brought them face to face with their hostess. The conventional handshake, the conventional words of greeting passed between that lady and Mrs. Romayne, and then the latter indicated Julian with a smiling gesture.

"Let me introduce my boy, Lady Arden," she said. "So glad to have the opportunity!"

She spoke with an accentuation of that self-conscious, self-deriding maternal pride which was her usual pose, setting, as it were, her tone for the night. And certainly Julian, as he bowed, and then shook the hand Lady Arden held out to him, was a legitimate subject for pride. His sense of the importance of the occasion had given to his manner and expression not only that touch of excitement which made him positively handsome, but a certain added readiness and assurance, by no means presuming and very attractive. Lady Arden's eyes rested on him with obvious approval, as she said the few words the situation demanded with unusual graciousness, and a sign from her brought one of her daughters to her side. She introduced Julian to the girl.

"Take care of Mr. Romayne, Ida," she said. "He has only lately come to London. Find him some nice partners."

"And let me have him back by-and-by, please, Lady Ida!" laughed Mrs. Romayne, as they passed on with the girl into the room. "There are some friends of his mother's to whom he must spare a little time to-night."

The gay replies with which Julian and his guide—who after a comprehensive glance at him had shown considerable readiness to do her mother's bidding—disappeared in the crowd were lost to Mrs. Romayne; her attention was claimed by a man at her elbow.

"May I have a dance, Mrs. Romayne?" he said.

Mrs. Romayne shook hands and laughed.

"Well, really I don't know," she said; "I think I must give up dancing from to-night. I've got a great grown-up son here, do you know. Look, there he is with Lady Ida Arden! Nice-looking boy, isn't he? It doesn't seem the right thing for his mother to be dancing about, now does it?"

She laughed again, a gay little laugh, well in the key she had set in her first introduction of Julian, and the man to whom she spoke protested vigorously.

"It seems to me exactly the right thing," he said. "The idea of your having a grown-up son is the preposterous point, don't you know. Come, I say, Mrs. Romayne, don't be so horribly hard-hearted!"

"But I must introduce him, don't you see. I must do my duty as a mother."

"Lady Ida is introducing him! She has introduced him to half-a-dozen of the best girls in the room already."

The colloquy, carried on on either side in the lightest of tones, finally ended in Mrs. Romayne's promising a "turn by-and-by," and the couple drifted apart; Mrs. Romayne to find acquaintances close at hand. Among the first she met was Lady Bracondale, condescendingly amiable, to whom she pointed out Julian, with laughing self-excuse. He was dancing now, and dancing extremely well.

"I am so absurdly proud of him!" she said. "I want to introduce him to you by-and-by, if I can catch him. But dancing men are so inconveniently useful."

Some time had worn away, and she had repeated the substance of this speech in sundry forms to sundry persons, before Julian rejoined her. She had cast several rather preoccupied glances in his direction, when she became aware of him on the opposite side of the room, threading his way through the intervening groups in her direction, just as she was accosted by a rather distinguished-looking, elderly man.

"How do you do, Mrs. Romayne? They tell me that you have a grown-up son here, and I decline to believe it."

He spoke in a pleasant, refined voice, marred, however, by all the affectation of the day, and with a tone about it as of a man absolutely secure of position and used to some amount of homage. He was a certain Lord Garstin, a distinguished figure in London society, rich, well-bred, and idle. He was troubled with no ideals. Fashionable women, with all the weaknesses which he knew quite well, were quite as high a type of woman as he thought possible; or, at least, desirable; and he had a considerable admiration for Mrs. Romayne as a very highly-finished and attractive specimen of the type he preferred.

She shook hands with him with a laugh, and a gathering together of her social resources, so to speak, which suggested that in her scheme of things he was a power whose suffrage was eminently desirable.

"It is true, notwithstanding," she said brightly. "I am the proud possessor of a grown-up son, Lord Garstin; a very dear boy, I assure you. We are settling down in London together."

"Is it possible?" was the answer, uttered with exaggerated incredulity. "And what are you going to do with him, may I ask?"

"He is reading for the bar——" began Mrs. Romayne; and then becoming aware that the subject of her words had by this time reached her side, she turned slightly, and laid her hand on Julian's arm with a pretty gesture. "Here he is," she said. "Let me introduce him. Julian, this is Lord Garstin. He has been kindly asking me about you."

Julian knew all about Lord Garstin, and his tone and manner as he responded to his mother's words were touched with a deference which made them, as his mother said to herself, "just what they ought to be." The elder man looked him over with eyes which, as far as their vision extended, were as keen as eyes need be.

"A great many of your mother's admirers will find it difficult to realise your existence," he said pleasantly. "Though of course we have all heard of you. You are going to the bar, eh?"

Lord Garstin had a great following among smart young men, and the fact was rather a weakness of his. He liked to have young men about him; to be admired and imitated by them. His manner to Julian was characteristic of these tastes; free from condescension as superiority can only be when it is absolute and unassailable, and full of easy familiarity.

Mrs. Romayne, standing fanning herself between them, listened for Julian's reply with a certain intent suspense beneath her smile; Lord Garstin's approval was so important to him. The simple, unaffected frankness of the answer satisfied her ear, and Lord Garstin's expression, as he listened to it, satisfied her eye; and with a laughing comment on Julian's words, she allowed her attention to be drawn away for the moment by an acquaintance who claimed it in passing.

There was a slight flush of elation on her face when, a few moments later, the chat between Lord Garstin and Julian being broken off, the former moved away with a friendly nod to the young man, and a little gesture and smile to herself, significant of congratulation.

"Come and walk round the room," she said gaily, slipping her hand through Julian's arm. "There are hundreds of people you must be introduced to."

During the half-hour that followed, Julian was introduced to a large proportion of those people in the room who were best worth knowing. Mrs. Romayne seemed to have wasted no time on the acquaintance of mediocrities.

His presentation to Lady Bracondale had just been accomplished, when Mrs. Halse appeared upon the scene and greeted Mrs. Romayne with stereotyped enthusiasm.

"Such a success!" she said in a loud whisper, as Julian talked to Lady Bracondale. "Everybody is quite taken by surprise. I don't know why, I'm sure, but I don't think any one was prepared for such a charming young man. I've been quite in love with him ever since I saw him first, you know, and we really must have him on the bazaar committee." Mrs. Halse had been out of town for Easter, and the affairs of the bazaar had been somewhat in abeyance in consequence. "Mr. Romayne," she continued, seizing upon Julian, "I want to talk to you. You really must help me——"

At this juncture the man who had pressed Mrs. Romayne to dance earlier in the evening came up to her and claimed the promise she had made him then. She cast a glance of laughing pity at Julian, intended for his eyes alone, and moved away.

"It was too bad, mother," he declared, laughing, as he met her a little later coming out of the dancing-room. "Now, to make up you must have one turn with me—just one. We haven't danced together for ages."

He was full of eagerness, a little flushed with the excitement of the evening, and her laughing protestations, her ridicule of him for wanting to dance with his mother, went for nothing. They only let loose on her a torrent of boyish persuasion, and finally she hesitated, laughed undecidedly, and yielded. She, too, was a little flushed and elated, as though with triumph.

"One turn, then, you absurd boy!" she said; and she let him draw her hand through his arm and lead her back into the dancing-room. They went only half-a-dozen times round the room in spite of his protestations against stopping, but Mrs. Romayne was too excellent a dancer and too striking a figure for those turns to pass unnoticed. When she stopped and made him take her, flushed and laughing, out of the room, she was instantly surrounded by a group of men vehemently reproaching her for dancing with her son to the exclusion of so many would-be partners, and laughingly denouncing Julian.

"I couldn't help it!" she protested gaily. "Yes, I know it's a ridiculous sight, but we are rather ridiculous, we two, you know! Come, Julian, take me home this moment! Let me disappear covered with confusion."

She went swiftly downstairs as she spoke, laughing prettily, and a few minutes later Julian, with a good deal of extraneous and wholly unnecessary assistance, was putting her into her carriage.

The whole evening had gone off admirably, Mrs. Romayne said the next morning; repeating the dictum with which she had parted from Julian at night, with less excitement, but with undiminished satisfaction.

During the course of the next three or four weeks that satisfaction—a certain genuine and deliberate satisfaction which seemed to underlie the superficial gaiety and brightness of her manner—seemed to grow upon her. The season had begun early, and very gaily, and she and Julian were in great request. It was perhaps as well that little work was expected of the embryo barrister before the winter, for he and his mother were out night after night; welcomed and made much of wherever they went, as so attractive a pair—one of whom was steeped to the finger-tips in knowledge of her world—were sure to be. Mrs. Romayne arranged a series of weekly dinner-parties in the little house at Chelsea, which promised to be, in a small way, one of the features of the season. They were very small, very select, and very cheery; no better hostess was to be found in London, and there was a touch of sentiment about the relation between the hostess and the pleasant young host, which was by no means without charm for the guests.

Mrs. Halse's bazaar, too, which was affording far more entertainment to its promoters than it seemed at all likely to afford to its supporters, served to bring Julian into special prominence. He was not clever, but there is a great deal to be done in connection with a bazaar on which intellect would be thrown away, and Julian proved himself what Mrs. Halse described effusively as "a most useful dear!" an expression by which she probably meant to convey the fact that he was always ready to toil for the ladies' committee, without too close an investigation into the end to be attained by the said toiling. He was quite an important person at all the meetings connected with the bazaar, and the fact gave him a standing with the innumerable "smart" people concerned which he would otherwise hardly have attained so soon.

His introduction to Lord Garstin resulted, about a fortnight after it took place, in an invitation to a bachelor dinner. An invitation to one of Lord Garstin's dinners was, in its way, about as desirable a thing as a young man "in Society" could receive; and the pleased, repressed importance on Julian's face as he came into the drawing-room to his mother before he started to keep the engagement, was like a faint reflection of the satisfaction with which Mrs. Romayne's expression was transfused.

"You're going?" she said brightly. "Well, I shall be at the Ponsonbys' by half-past eleven, and I shall expect you there some time before twelve. Enjoy yourself, sir!"

He kissed her with careless affection, and she patted him on the shoulder for a conceited boy as he hoped, lightly, that she would not find her solitary evening dull; she had refused to dine out without him, saying laughingly that she should enjoy a holiday; and then he went off, whistling gaily and arranging his buttonhole.

It wanted a few minutes only to the dinner-hour when he arrived at the club where the dinner was to be given. Three of his fellow guests were already assembled, and to two of these—well-known young men about town—he had already been introduced.

"You know these two fellows, I think," said Lord Garstin lightly, "but"—turning to the third man—"Loring tells me that you and he have not yet been introduced. I'm delighted to perform the ceremony! Mr. Julian Romayne—Mr. Marston Loring!"

Julian held out his hand with a frank exclamation of pleasure. He had recognised in Mr. Marston Loring a young man whom he had seen about incessantly during the past month, and who had excited a good deal of secret and boyish admiration in him by reason of a certain assumption of *blasé* cynicism with which an excellent society manner was just sufficiently seasoned to give it character. It was conventional character enough, but it was not to be expected that Julian should understand that.

"I'm awfully glad to meet you," he said pleasantly. "I've known you by sight for ages!"

"And I you!" was the answer, spoken with a slight smile and a touch of cordiality which delighted Julian. "The pleasure is distinctly mutual."

Marston Loring was not a good-looking young man; his features, indeed, would have been insignificant but for the presence of that spurious air of refinement which life in society usually produces; and for something more genuine, namely, a strength and resolution about the mould of his chin and the set of his thin lips which had won him a reputation for being "cleverlooking" among the superficial observers of the social world. He was nine-and-twenty, but his face might have been the face of a man twenty years older—so entirely destitute was it of any of the gracious possibilities which should characterise early manhood. It was pale and lined, and worn with very ugly suggestiveness; and there were stories told about him, whispered and laughed at in many of the houses where he was received, which accounted amply for those lines. The pose, too, which it pleased him to adopt was that of elderly superiority to all the illusions and credulities of youth. Marston Loring was a man of whom it was vaguely but universally said that he had "got on so well!" Reduced to facts, this statement meant, primarily, that with no particular rights in that direction he had gradually worked his way into a position in society—a position the insecurity and unreality of which was known only to himself; and, secondarily, that by dint of influence, hard work—hard work was also part of his pose—and a certain amount of unscrupulousness, he was making money at the bar when most men dependent on their profession would have starved at it.

He had brown eyes, dull and curiously shallow-looking, but very keen and calculating, and they were even keener than usual as they gave Julian one quick look.

"I think we belong to the same profession?" he said with easy friendliness. "You are reading with Allardyce, are you not? A good man, Allardyce."

"So they tell me," answered Julian, not a little impressed by the critical and experienced tone of the approbation. "I can't say I've done much with him yet. One doesn't do much at this time of year, you know."

Loring smiled rather sardonically.

"That's what it is to be a gentleman of independent fortune," he said. "Some people have to burn the candle at both ends."

The five minutes' chat which ensued before the arrival of the fifth guest—a certain Lord Hesseltine, known only by sight to Julian—and the announcement of dinner, was just enough to create a regret in Julian's mind when he found that he and his new acquaintance were seated on opposite sides of the table. Loring's contribution to the general conversation throughout dinner, witty, cynical, and assured, completed his conquest, and when, on the subsequent adjournment of the party to the smoking-room, Loring strolled up to him, cigar in hand, the prospect of a *tête-à-tête* was greatly to Julian's satisfaction.

"What an odd thing it is that we should never have been introduced before!" he began, lighting his own cigar and scanning the other man with youthful, admiring eyes.

"It is odd," returned Loring placidly, throwing himself into an arm-chair as he spoke, and signing an invitation to Julian to establish himself in another. "Especially as, like every one else, I've been an immense admirer of your mother all this year. I wonder whether you recognise what a lucky fellow you are, Romayne?"

Julian's eyes sparkled with pleasure at the easy familiarity of the address, and he crossed his legs with careless self-importance, as he answered, with the lightness of youth:

"I ought to, oughtn't I? I say, I know my mother would be awfully pleased to know you. You must let me introduce you to her. Are you coming on to the Ponsonbys' to-night?"

"I shall be only too delighted," answered Loring, watching the smoke from his cigar with his dull, brown eyes, and answering the first part of Julian's speech. "No, unfortunately I've got an affair in Chelsea to-night, and another in Kensington. But we shall meet to-morrow night at the Bracondales', I suppose?"

"Of course," assented Julian eagerly. "That will be capital!"

There was a moment's pause, broken by Loring with a reference to a political opinion formulated by one of the other men at dinner; and a talk about politics ensued, eager on Julian's part, cynical and effectively reserved on Loring's. A political discussion, when the discussers hold the same political faith, has much the same effect in promoting rapid intimacy between men, granted a predisposition towards intimacy on either side, as a discussion of the reigning fashion in dress has with a certain class of women. When Lord Garstin's dinner-party began to break up, and Loring and Julian rose to take their departure, they parted with a hand-clasp which would have befitted an acquaintanceship three months, rather than three hours old.

"Good night," said Julian. "Awfully pleased to have met you, Loring. See you to-morrow night. My mother will be delighted."

"I shall be delighted," said Loring. "All right, then. To-morrow night we'll arrange that look in at the House. Good night."

A few minutes' talk with Lord Garstin, who had taken a decided fancy to "that charming little woman's boy," and Julian was standing on the pavement of St. James's Street, with that pleasant sense of exhilaration and warmth of heart, which is an attendant, in youth, on the inauguration of a new friendship.

It was a night in early May, and a fine, hot day had ended, as evening drew on, in sultry closeness. The clouds had been rolling up steadily, though not a breath of air seemed to be stirring now, and it was evident that a storm was inevitable before long. Julian was hot and excited; he had only a short distance to go; he looked up at the sky and decided—the wish being father to the thought—that it would "hold up for the present," and that he would walk.

He set out up St. James's Street and along Piccadilly, taking the right road by instinct, his busy thoughts divided between satisfaction at the idea of belonging to the "best" club in London, introduced thereinto by Lord Garstin; and Loring and his gifts and graces. He had just turned into Berkeley Street when a rattling peal of thunder roused him with a start, and the next instant the thunder was followed by a perfect deluge of rain.

It was so sudden and he was so entirely unprepared, that his only instinct for the moment was to step back hastily into the shelter of a portico in front of which he was just passing; and as he did so, he noticed a young woman who must have been following him up the street, a young woman in the shabby hat and jacket of a work-girl, take refuge, perforce, beneath the same shelter with a shrinking movement which was not undignified, though it seemed to imply that she was almost more afraid of him than of the drenching, bitter rain. Then, his reasoning powers reasserting themselves in the comparative security of the portico, he began to consider what he should do. He was within seven minutes' walk of his destination, but seven minutes' walk in such rain as was beating down on the pavement before him would render him wholly unfit to present himself at a party; and "of course," as he said to himself, there was not a cab to be seen. A blinding flash of lightning cut across his reflections, and drove him back a step or two farther into shelter involuntarily. And as a terrific peal of thunder followed it instantaneously, he glanced almost unconsciously at the sharer of his shelter.

"By Jove!" he said to himself.

The girl had retreated, as he himself had done, and was standing close up against the door of the house to which the portico belonged, in the extreme corner from that which he himself occupied. But except for that tacit acknowledgement of his presence, she seemed no longer conscious of it. She was looking straight out at the storm, her head a little lifted as though to catch a glimpse of the sky; and her face, outlined by her dark clothes and the dark paint of the door behind her, stood out in great distinctness. It was rather thin and pale, and very tired-looking; the large brown eyes were heavy and haggard. It was not worthy of a second glance at that moment, according to any canon of the world in which Julian lived, and yet it drew from him that exclamation of startled admiration. He had never seen anything like it, he told himself vaguely.

Apparently the intent gaze, of which he himself was hardly conscious, affected its object. She moved uneasily, and turning as if involuntarily, met his eyes.

The next instant she was moving hastily from under the portico, when the driver of a hansom cab became aware of Julian's existence, and pulled up suddenly.

"Hansom, sir?" he shouted.

"Yes!" answered Julian quickly, dashing across the drenched pavement. "A hundred and three, Berkeley Square!"

CHAPTER X

ALL the rooms in the house in Chelsea were bright and pretty, and by no means the least attractive was the dining-room. The late breakfast-hour fixed by Mrs. Romayne, "just for the season," as she said, gave plenty of time for the sun to find its way in at the windows; and on the morning following Julian's dinner with Lord Garstin the sunshine was dancing on the walls, and the soft, warm air floating in at the open windows, as though the thunderstorm of the previous evening had cleared the air to some purpose.

The two occupants of the room, as they faced one another across the dainty little breakfast-table, had been laughing and talking after their usual fashion ever since they sat down; talking of the party of the night before and of engagements in the future; and finally reverting to Lord Garstin's dinner and Marston Loring, of whom Julian had already had a great deal to say.

"I have a kind of feeling that he and I are going to be chums, mother!" he said as he carried his coffee-cup round the table to her to be refilled. "I think he took to me rather, do you know!"

"That's a very surprising thing, isn't it?" returned his mother, laughing. "And you took to him? Well, if you must pick up a chum, you couldn't do it under better auspices than Lord Garstin's."

"I took to him no end!" answered Julian eagerly. "I do hope you'll like him."

"I think I am pretty sure to like him," said Mrs. Romayne graciously. "I remember hearing about him some time ago—that he was quite one of the rising young men of the day. He was to have been introduced to me then. I forget why it didn't come off. There's your coffee!"

Julian took his cup with a word of thanks and turned back to his chair; and his mother began again.

"Mr. Loring is a member of the Prince's, I suppose?" she said. The "Prince's" was the name of the club at which Lord Garstin's dinner had been given. "I suppose you will want to be setting up a club in no time, sir?"

Julian laughed, and then replied somewhat eagerly and confidentially, as though in unconscious response to a certain invitation in his mother's tone.

"Well, of course a fellow does want a club, mother," he said. "One feels it more and more, don't you know! Of course I should awfully like to belong to the Prince's."

"And why not?" responded his mother brightly, watching him rather narrowly as she spoke. "Lord Garstin would put you up, I've no doubt, if I asked him."

Julian's eyes sparkled.

"It would be first-rate!" he exclaimed. "Mother, it's awfully jolly of you!" He paused a moment and then continued tentatively: "It would be rather expensive, you know. That's the only thing!"

"So I suppose!" answered his mother, laughing. "Oh, you're a very expensive luxury altogether! However, I imagine another hundred a year would do?" Then as he broke into vehement demonstrations of delight and gratitude, she added with another laugh which did not seem to ring quite true: "I don't think you need ever run short of money!"

There was a moment's pause as Julian, the picture of glowing satisfaction, finished his breakfast, and then Mrs. Romayne rose.

"What are you going to do this morning?" she said. "Read?"

Julian glanced out of the window.

"Well," he said, "it's an awfully jolly morning, isn't it? I promised to see after some live-stock for Miss Pomeroy's stall—puppies, and kittens, and canary birds. Rum idea, isn't it? What are you doing this morning, dear?"

It turned out that Mrs. Romayne had nothing particular on her hands beyond a visit to a jeweller in Bond Street, and accepting very easily his substitution of Miss Pomeroy's commission for the legal studies to which he was supposed to devote himself in the mornings, she took up his reference to the weather, and suggested that they should drive together to execute first his business and then her own.

"It will be rather nice driving this morning," she said. "And we can take a turn in the Park."

Certainly there was a certain amount of excuse for those people who had already begun to say that Mrs. Romayne was never happy without her son by her side.

She spared no pains, however, to make him happy with her; and as they drove along there was probably no brighter or brisker talk than theirs in progress in all London. They drove through the West End streets and penetrated, in search of Miss Pomeroy's requirements, into regions into which Mrs. Romayne had hardly ever penetrated before; regions which rather amused her to-day in their squalor. When Julian had done his commission in plenty of time to undo it and do it again before the bazaar came off, as he remarked with a laugh, they turned back again and went to Bond Street.

"I have a little private matter to attend to here," said Julian, as he followed his mother into the jeweller's shop. "You just have the kindness to stop at your end of the shop, will you, please, and leave me to mine?"

Mrs. Romayne laughed and shook her head at him. It was within a few days of her birthday, which was always demonstratively honoured by her son.

"Now, you are not to be extravagant," she said, holding up a slender, threatening finger with mock severity. "Mind, I will not have it. I shall descend upon you unawares, and keep you in order."

She let him leave her with another laugh, and he disappeared to the other end of the shop, while she followed a shopman to a counter near the door. Just turning away from it, she met Mrs. Pomeroy and her daughter.

"Now, this is really most delightful!" exclaimed Mrs. Pomeroy, if any speech so comfortable and so entirely unexcited may be described as an exclamation. "It is always charming to see you, dear Mrs. Romayne, of course; but it really is particularly charming this morning, isn't it, Maud?"

"That's very nice," said Mrs. Romayne brightly, turning to Maud Pomeroy with a smile, and pressing the girl's hand with an affectionate familiarity developed in her with regard to Miss Pomeroy by the last few weeks. A hardly perceptible touch of additional satisfaction had come to her face as she saw the mother and daughter. "Please tell me why?"

"Yes, of course," said Mrs. Pomeroy placidly; she sat down as she spoke with that instinct for personal ease under all circumstances, which was her ruling characteristic. "That is just what I want to do. My dear Mrs. Romayne, it is the bazaar, of course. It really is a most awkward thing, isn't it, Maud? It seems that we have asked twenty-one ladies—all most important—to become stall-holders, and we can't possibly make room for more than eighteen stalls! Now, what would you—— Ah, Mr. Romayne, how do you do?"

Mrs. Pomeroy had broken off her tale of woe as placidly as she had begun it, and had greeted Julian with comfortable cordiality. He had come up hastily, not becoming aware of his mother's companions until he was close to them.

"This is awfully lucky for me!" he exclaimed. "I want a lady desperately for half a minute, and my mother won't do. Miss Pomeroy," turning eagerly to the demure, correct-looking figure standing by Mrs. Pomeroy's side, "will you come to the other end of the shop with me for half a minute? It would be awfully good of you."

The words were spoken in a tone of fashionable good-fellowship—the pseudo good-fellowship which passes for the real thing in society—which, as addressed by Julian Romayne to Miss Pomeroy and her mother, was one of the results of his work in connection with the bazaar; and before Miss Pomeroy could answer, Mrs. Romayne interposed. Somebody very frequently did interpose when Miss Pomeroy was addressed. No one ever seemed to expect opinions or decisions from her; perhaps because she was her mother's daughter; perhaps because of her curiously characterless exterior; while the fact that she had never been known to controvert a statement—in words—doubtless accentuated the tendency of her acquaintance to make statements for her.

"It will be awfully good of you," Mrs. Romayne said to her now, laughing, "if you are kind enough to help this silly fellow, to insist on his remembering that his mother will be very angry indeed if he is extravagant. I shall have to give up having a birthday, I think."

Then as Julian, with a gay gesture of repression to his mother, waited for Miss Pomeroy's answer with another pleading, "It would be ever so good of you," the girl, with a glance at her mother, said, with a conventional smile, "With pleasure," and walked away by his side.

Mrs. Pomeroy looked after Julian with an approving smile. He was a favourite of hers.

"Such a nice fellow," she murmured amiably; and Mrs. Romayne laughed her pretty, self-conscious laugh.

"So glad you find him so," she said. "Oh, by-the-bye, dear Mrs. Pomeroy, can you tell me anything about a Mr. Marston Loring? He goes everywhere, doesn't he? I think I have seen him at your house."

"Oh, yes," returned Mrs. Pomeroy, as placidly as ever, but with a decision which indicated that she was giving expression to a popular verdict, not merely to an opinion of her own. "He is quite a young man to know. Very clever, and rising. I don't know what his people were; he has been so successful that it really doesn't signify, you know. He lives in chambers—I don't remember where, but it is a very good address."

"Has he money?" asked Mrs. Romayne.

"I really don't know," said Mrs. Pomeroy. "He is doing extremely well at the bar. By the way, they say," and herewith Mrs. Pomeroy lowered her voice and confided to her interlocutor two or three details in connection with Marston Loring's private life—the life which in the world no one is supposed to recognise—which might have been considered by no means to his credit. They were not details which affected his society character in any way, however, and Mrs. Romayne only laughed with such slight affectation of reprobation as a woman of the world should show.

"Men are all alike, I suppose," she said, with that fashionable indulgence which has probably done as much as anything else towards making men "all alike." "By-the-bye, he was Lord Dunstan's best man, wasn't he?"

Mrs. Pomeroy was just confirming to Mr. Marston Loring what was evidently a certificate of social merit, when Julian and Miss Pomeroy reappeared, and Mrs. Romayne, with an exclamation at herself as a "frightful gossip," turned to the shopman, who had been waiting her pleasure at a discreet distance, and transacted her business.

"We haven't settled anything about this trying business of the twenty-one stall-holders," said Mrs. Pomeroy plaintively, as she finished. "Now, I wonder—we were thinking of taking a turn in the Park, weren't we, Maud?" Mrs. Pomeroy had a curious little habit of constantly referring to her daughter. "It would be so kind of you, dear Mrs. Romayne, if you would send your carriage home and take a turn with us, you and Mr. Romayne, and I would take you home, of course. I really am anxious to know what you advise, for there seems to be an idea that I am in some way responsible for the awkwardness. So absurd, you know. I am quite sure I have only done as I was told."

Apparently it had not occurred to Mrs. Pomeroy that to do as you are told by four or five different people with totally different ends in view is apt to lead to confusion.

Mrs. Romayne fell in with the plan proposed, after an instant's demur, with smiling alacrity, and the "turn in the Park" that followed was a very gay one. Miss Pomeroy and Julian laughed and talked together—that is to say, Julian laughed and talked in the best of good spirits, and Miss Pomeroy put in just the correct words and pretty smiles which were wanted to keep his conversation in full swing. Mrs. Romayne and Mrs. Pomeroy, facing them, disposed of the difficulty in connection with the bazaar, after a good deal of irrelevant discussion, by saying very often, and in a great many words, that three more stalls must be got in somewhere; a decision which seemed to Mrs. Pomeroy to make everything perfectly right, although she had had it elaborately demonstrated to her that such a course was absolutely impossible.

It was half-past one when Mrs. Romayne and Julian were put down at their own door, and the barouche drove off amid a chorus of light laughter and last words. The sunshine, the fresh air, the movement, or something less simple and less physical, seemed to have had a most exhilarating effect on Mrs. Romayne. Her face was almost as radiant in its curiously different fashion as Julian's was radiant with the unreasoning good spirits of youth.

"Such nice people!" she said lightly. "I wonder whether lunch is ready? I'm quite starving! Oh, letters!" taking up three or four which lay on the hall-table. "Let us trust they are interesting!" She turned into the dining-room as she spoke, sorting the envelopes in her hand. "One for you—your friend Von Mühler, isn't it?" she said, tossing it to Julian carelessly. "One for me—

an invitation obviously. One from Mrs. Ponsonby, about her stall, I suppose. And one from——"

She stopped suddenly. The last letter of the pile was contained in a small square envelope, and addressed in what was obviously a man's handwriting—a good handwriting, clear and strong, but somewhat cramped and precise. "Mrs. William Romayne, 22, Queen Anne Street, Chelsea." A curious stillness seemed to come over the little alert figure as the pale blue eyes caught sight of the writing, and then Mrs. Romayne moved and walked slowly away to the window, still with her eyes fixed on the envelope. She paused a moment, and then she opened it and drew out a sheet of note-paper bearing a few lines only in the same small, clear hand.

"Well, mother, and what have your correspondents got to say? I have had no end of a screed from Von Mühler."

Nearly ten minutes had passed, and Mrs. Romayne started violently. She thrust the letter—still open in her hand, though she was looking fixedly out of the window—back into its envelope and turned. Her face had altered curiously and completely. All its colour, all the genuine animation which had pervaded it as she came into the room, had disappeared; it was pale and hard-looking, and the lines about the mouth and eyes were very visible.

"A dinner invitation from Lady Ashton," she said, "and a long rigmarole from Mrs. Ponsonby to tell me that she is resigning her stall, and why she is doing it. Poor Mrs. Pomeroy should be grateful to her!"

Her tone was an exaggeration of her bright carelessness of ten minutes before, forced and unnatural; her back was towards the window, or even Julian's boyish eyes might have noticed the stiff unreality of the smile with which she spoke.

They sat down to lunch together, but the strange change which had come to her did not pass away. Julian did most of the talking, though the readiness of her comments and her smiles—which left her lips always hard and set, and never seemed to touch her eyes—prevented his being in the least aware of the fact. Their afternoon was spent apart; but when they met again there was that about her face which made Julian say with some surprise:

"Are you tired, mother?"

They were going to a large dinner-party before the very smart "at home" to which Julian and Mr. Loring had referred on the previous evening as an opportunity for meeting, and Mrs. Romayne was magnificently dressed. There were diamonds round her throat and in her hair, and as they flashed and sparkled, seeming to lend glow and animation to her face as she laughed at him for a ridiculous boy, Julian thought carelessly that he must have imagined the drawn look which had struck him—though he had only recognised it as "tired-looking"—on his mother's face. As though his words had startled or even annoyed her, she gave neither Julian nor any one else any further excuse for taxing her with fatigue. Throughout the long and rather dull dinner she was vivacity itself; her face always smiling, her laugh always ready. As the evening went on a flush made its appearance on her cheeks, as though the mental stimulus under which that gaiety was produced involved a veritable quickening of the pulses; and her son, when he met her in the hall after she had uncloaked for their second party, thought that he had never seen his mother look "jollier," as he expressed it.

"We must look out for Loring," he said eagerly. "Oh, there he is, mother, just inside the doorway! That clever-looking fellow, do you see, with a yellow buttonhole?"

It was easier to recognise an acquaintance than to approach within speaking distance of him; and some time elapsed, during which Mrs. Romayne and Julian exchanged greetings on all sides, and were received by Lady Bracondale, before they found themselves also just inside the doorway. Mrs. Romayne had given one quick, keen glance in the direction indicated by Julian, and then had become apparently oblivious of Mr. Marston Loring's existence until Julian finally exclaimed:

"Well met, Loring! Awfully pleased to see you! Mother, may I introduce Mr. Marston Loring?"

She turned her head then, and bent it very graciously, holding out her hand with her most charming smile.

"I have known you by sight for a long time, Mr. Loring!" she said. "I am delighted to make your acquaintance!"

"The delight is mine!" was the response, spoken with just that touch of well-bred deference which is never so attractive to a woman as when it is exhibited in conjunction with such a personality as Loring's. "It is one for which I have wished for a long time!"

"Seen the papers to-night?" interposed Julian eagerly. "We've lost Nottingham, you see!"

He was alluding to a bye-election which had led to the political discussion of the evening before, and Loring nodded.

"I see," said Loring. "Romayne has told you, no doubt," he went on, turning to Mrs. Romayne, "that we foregathered to a considerable extent last night over politics—and other things." The last words were spoken with a glance at the younger man which seemed to ascribe to their acquaintance an altogether more personal and friendly footing than political discussion alone could have afforded it, and Mrs. Romayne laughed very graciously.

"Yes; he has told me!" she said. "I am rather thinking of getting a little jealous of you, Mr. Loring."

A few minutes' more talk followed—talk in which Loring bore himself with his usual cynical manner, just tempered into even unusual effectiveness—and then Mrs. Romayne prepared to move on.

"You must come and see us," she said to Loring. "Julian will give you the address. I am at home on Fridays; and I hope you will dine with us before long!"

She gave him a pretty nod and an "*au revoir*," and turned away.

"He's awfully jolly, isn't he, mother?" exclaimed Julian, as soon as they were out of earshot.

"Very good style," returned Mrs. Romayne approvingly. "He is just the kind of man to get on. You have a good deal of discrimination, sir," she added.

The mother and son were separated after that, and about half an hour later Mrs. Romayne caught sight of Julian disappearing with a very pretty girl, whose face she did not know, in the direction of the supper-room, just as she herself was greeted by Lord Garstin and pressed to repair thither.

"Thanks, no," she said lightly. "There is such a crowd, and I really don't want anything."

She paused. That accentuated vivacity was still about her, as she looked up at Lord Garstin with a little smile and a gesture which he thought unusually charming.

"I want a little chat with you, though, very much," she said with pretty confidence. "I'm going to ask you to give me some advice, do you know. Will it bore you frightfully?"

"On the contrary, it will delight me," was the ready and by no means insincere response.

Mrs. Romayne made a gracious and grateful movement of her head.

"I would rather take your opinion than that of any other man I know," she said confidentially. She stopped and laughed slightly. "It's about my boy, of course!" she said. "I want to know what you think of a club for a young man in his position? Do you think, now, that it is a good thing?"

"Emphatically, yes," returned Lord Garstin. "I consider a good club of the first importance to a young man. Your young man ought to be a member of the Prince's." He paused a moment, looking at her as she nodded her head softly, waiting as though for further words of wisdom from him, and thought what a delightful little woman she was. "Suppose I talk to him about it?" he said pleasantly. "I will see to it with pleasure if you would like it."

Nothing, certainly, could have been more delightful than Mrs. Romayne's manner, as she spoke just the right words of graceful acknowledgement and acceptance. Then she made a gaily disparaging comment on club life, and Lord Garstin's advocacy of it, and a few minutes' bantering, laughing repartee followed—that society repartee of which Mrs. Romayne was a mistress. From thence she drifted into talk about the party, and a complaint of the heat of the room.

"It is time we were going, I think!" she remarked, with a gay little laugh. "But a mother is a miserable slave, you see! I am 'left until called for,' I suppose!"

"If I were not absolutely obliged to go myself," returned Lord Garstin, "I shouldn't encourage such a suggestion on your part. But as that is the case, unfortunately, shall I find your boy first and send him to you?"

Mrs. Romayne shook her head with another laugh.

"I saw him retire to the supper-room a little while ago with a very pretty girl," she said. "I make it a point never to hurry him under such circumstances! But if you should meet him you might tell him that I am quite ready when he is. Good night!"

The room was not by any means crowded now; it was getting late and a great many people were in the supper-room. The corner of the room in which Mrs. Romayne was standing happened to be nearly deserted; there was no one near her, and after Lord Garstin left her, she stood still, fanning herself and looking straight before her with her bright smile and animated expression rather stereotyped on her face. Suddenly, as if involuntarily, she turned her head; she looked across to the other side of the room and met the eyes of a man standing against the wall, who had been looking fixedly at her ever since Lord Garstin joined her. For an instant not the slightest perceptible change of expression touched her face; only the very absoluteness of its immobility suggested that that immobility was the result of a sudden and tremendous effort of self-control; then the colour faded slowly from her cheeks and from her lips; the smile did not disappear but it gradually assumed a ghastly appearance of being carved in marble; her eyes widened slightly and became strangely fixed. The man was Dennis Falconer, and he and she were looking at one another across the gulf of eighteen years.

It was only for a moment. Then Mrs. Romayne, still quite colourless, lifted her eyebrows prettily and made a gesture of amazed recognition, and Falconer moved and came slowly towards her.

"What a surprising thing!" she exclaimed, holding out her hand. "I had no idea you were here to-night! How do you do? Welcome home!"

Her tone was perfectly easy and gracious; so ultra-easy, indeed, that it deprived her words of any personal or emotional significance whatever, and relegated their meeting-place with subtle skill to the most conventional of society grounds. The rather distinguished-looking man with the good reserved manner who stood before her accepted the position with grave readiness.

"Thank you," he said. He spoke with distant courtesy, about which there was not even the suggestion of that matter-of-course friendliness, as of distant kinship, which had made her reception of him nearly perfect as a work of art. "It is a great pleasure to me to be in England again."

"You have been away—let me see—two years?" said Mrs. Romayne, with the vivacious assumption of intelligent interest which the social situation demanded. "Five, is it? Really? And you have done wonderful things, I hear. Funnily enough, I have been hearing about you only to-night. I must congratulate you."

He bent his head with a courteous gesture of thanks.

"You have had my note, I hope?" he said. "You are settled in London now, Thomson tells me."

Thomson was the family lawyer, and he and Dennis Falconer himself were Mrs. Romayne's trustees under old Mr. Falconer's will.

"Oh, yes!" she answered suavely. "I had it to-day, just before lunch. So nice of you to write to me. Yes, we are settled——"

She had been fanning herself carelessly throughout the short colloquy, glancing at Falconer or about the room with every appearance of perfect ease; but now, as her eyes wandered to the other end of the room something seemed to catch her attention. She hesitated, appeared to forget what she had intended to say, tried to recover herself, and failed.

Julian had come into the room, and was just parting gaily from some one in the doorway. Dennis Falconer did not take up her unfinished sentence; he followed the direction of her eyes across the room until his own rested upon Julian, and then he started slightly and glanced down at the woman by his side.

Mrs. Romayne laughed a rather high, unnatural laugh. She faced him with her eyes very hard and bright, and her lips smiling; and through all the artificiality of her face and manner there was something lurking in those hard, bright eyes as she did it, something not to be caught or defined, which made the movement almost heroic.

"You recognise him?" she said lightly. "Ridiculously like me, isn't he?"

At that moment Julian started across the room, evidently to come to his mother. He came on, stopping incessantly to exchange good-nights, laughing, bowing, and smiling; and, as though there were a fascination for them about his gay young figure, the man and woman standing together at the other end of the room watched him draw nearer and nearer. Words continued to come from Mrs. Romayne, a pretty, inconsequent flow of society chatter, but it no more tempered the strange gaze with which her eyes followed her son than did the unheeding silence with which Falconer received them as his grave eyes rested also on the young man. The whole thing was so incongruous; the expression of those two pair of eyes was so utterly out of harmony with their surroundings, and with the laughing, unconscious boy on whom they were fixed; that they seemed to draw him out from the brightly dressed, smiling groups through which he passed, and isolate him strangely in a weird atmosphere of his own.

"Here you are, sir!" cried his mother gaily, looking no longer at Julian as he stood close to her at last, but beyond him.

"Lord Garstin told me you were ready to go, dear," said Julian pleasantly. "I hope I haven't kept you?"

"There was no hurry," she answered, smiling; her voice was a little thin and strained. "We will go now, I think, but I want to introduce you first to some one whose name you know. This is your cousin, Dennis Falconer."

CHAPTER XI

It was a rather close afternoon in the third week of May. Fine weather had lasted without a break for more than a fortnight; for the last two or three days there had been little or no breeze; and the inevitable effect had been produced upon London. The streets were a combination of dust, which defied the water-carts; and glare, which seemed to radiate alike from the heavy, smoky-blue sky, the houses, and the pavements. It was only half-past three, and Piccadilly was as yet far from being crowded. The pavement was mainly occupied by the working population, which hurries to and fro along the London streets from morning to night regardless of fashionable hours; and the few representatives of the non-working class—smartly-dressed women and carefully got-up and sauntering men—stood out with peculiar distinctness. But the figure of Dennis Falconer, as he walked westward along the north side of Piccadilly, was conspicuous not only on these rather unenviable terms.

At the first glance it would have seemed that the past eighteen years had altered him considerably, and altered him always for the better; analysed carefully, the alteration resolved itself into a very noticeable increase of maturity and of a certain kind of strength; and the improvement into the fact that his weak points were of a kind to be far less perceptible as such on a mature than on an immature face. His face was thin and very brown; there were worn lines about it which told of physical endurance; and in the sharper chiselling of the whole the thinness of the nose and the narrowness of the forehead were no longer striking. The somewhat self-conscious superiority of his younger days had disappeared under the hand of time, and a certain sternness which had replaced it seemed to give dignity to his expression. The keen steadiness of his eyes had strengthened, and, indeed, it was their expression which helped in a very great degree to make his face so noticeable. He no longer wore a beard, and the firm, square outline of his chin and jaw were visible, while his mouth was hidden by a moustache; iron-grey like his hair. He was very well dressed, but there was that about the simple conventionality of his attire which suggested that its correctness was rather a concession to exterior demands than the expression of personal weakness.

More than one of the people who turned their heads to look at him as he walked down Piccadilly were familiar with that grave, stern face; it had been reproduced lately in the pages of all the illustrated papers, and people glanced at it with the interest created by the appearance in the flesh of something of a celebrity. Falconer had done a great deal of good work for the Geographical Society in the course of the past eighteen years; work characterised by no brilliancy or originality of intellectual resource, but eminently persevering, conscientious, and patient. During the last year, however, a chapter of accidents had conspired to invest the expedition of which he was the leader with a touch of romance and excitement with which his personality would never have endued it. The achievement in which the expedition had resulted had been hailed in England as a national triumph, and Dennis Falconer found himself one of the lions of the moment.

But the position, especially for a man who believed himself to attach no value whatever to it, had been somewhat dearly bought. Falconer, as he walked the London streets on that May afternoon, was trying to realise himself as at home in them, settled among them, perhaps, for an indefinite period; and the effort brought an added shade of gravity to his face. The terrible physical strain of the last six months; a strain the severity of which he had hardly realised at the time, as he endured from day to day with the simple, unimaginative perseverance of a man for whom nerves have no existence; had told even upon his iron constitution; and a couple of great London doctors had condemned him to a year's inactivity at least, under penalties too grave to be provoked.

He turned down Sloane Street, and another quarter of an hour brought him to number twenty-two, Queen Anne Street. He rang, was admitted, and ushered upstairs into the drawing-room.

The room was empty, and Falconer walked across it, glancing about him with those keen, habitually observant eyes of his, and on his face there was something of the stiffness and reserve which had characterised his voice a minute earlier as he asked for Mrs. Romayne.

Until the night, now nearly a fortnight ago, when they had met in Lady Bracondale's drawing-room, Dennis Falconer had seen Mrs. Romayne only once since their journey from Nice had ended in old Mr. Falconer's house. That one occasion had been his visit to his uncle—so called—in his Swiss home in the second year of Mrs. Romayne's widowhood.

He had been in Europe several times since then and had always made a point of visiting old Mr. Falconer, but on every subsequent occasion it had happened—rather strangely, as he had thought to himself once or twice—that Mrs. Romayne was away from home. After old Mr. Falconer's death communication between them occurred only at the rarest intervals. Dennis Falconer was Mrs. Romayne's only remaining relation, and in this capacity had been left by her uncle one of her trustees; but any necessary business was transacted by his fellow trustee—old Mr. Falconer's lawyer. But the clan instinct was very strong in Falconer; it brought in its wake a whole set of duties and obligations which for most men are non-existent; and the sense of duty which had been characteristic of him in early manhood had only been more deeply—and narrowly—engraved by every succeeding year.

Arrived in London, and knowing Mrs. Romayne to be settled there, he had considered it incumbent on him to call on her, and had written the note which she had received nearly a fortnight ago. He had written it with much the same expression on his face—only a little less pronounced, perhaps—as rested on it now that he was waiting for Mrs. Romayne in her own drawing-room. Through all the changes brought about by the passing of eighteen years, the mental attitude produced in him towards Mrs. Romayne during those weeks of dual solitude at Nice had remained almost untouched, except inasmuch as its disapproval had been accentuated by everything he had heard of her since. It had been vivified and rendered, as it were, tangible and definite by the short interview at Lady Bracondale's party, which had made her a reality instead of a remembrance to him.

He was standing before a large and very admirable photograph of Julian—Julian at his very best and most attractive—contemplating it with a heavy frown, when the door behind him opened under a light, quick touch, and Mrs. Romayne came into the room.

"It is too shocking to have kept you waiting!" she said. "So glad to see you! I gave myself too much shopping to do, and I have had quite a fearful rush!"

Her voice and manner were very easy, very conventionally cordial; and, as it seemed to Falconer, there was not a natural tone or movement about her. It was her "at home" afternoon, and she was charmingly dressed in something soft and pale-coloured; her eyes were very bright, and the play of expression on her face was even more vivacious and effective than usual—exaggeratedly so, even.

She shook hands and pointed him to a seat, sinking into a chair herself with an affectation of hard-won victory over the "fearful rush"; the subtle assumption of the most superficial society relation as alone existing between them was as insidious and as indefinable as it had been on their previous meeting, and seemed to set the key-note of the situation even before she spoke again.

"It is a frightful season!" she said. "Really horribly busy! They say it is to be a short one—I am sure I trust it is true, if we are any of us to be left alive at the end—and everything seems to be crammed into a few weeks. Don't you think so? You are very lucky to have arrived half-way through."

"London just now does not seem to be a particularly desirable place, certainly," answered Falconer; his manner was very formal and reserved, a great contrast to her apparent ease.

"No!" she said, lifting her eyebrows with a smile. "Now, that sounds rather ungrateful in you, do you know, for London finds you a very desirable visitor. One hears of you everywhere."

"I am afraid I must confess that I take very little pleasure in going 'everywhere,'" returned Falconer stiffly. "Social life in London seems to me to have altered for the worse in every direction, since I last took part in it."

"And yet you go out a great deal!" with a laugh. "That sounds a trifle inconsistent!"

"I am not sufficiently egotistical to imagine that my individual refusal to countenance it would have any effect upon society," answered Falconer, still more stiffly. "To tolerate is by no means to approve."

Falconer's reasons for the toleration in question—the real reasons, of which he himself was wholly unconscious—would have astonished him not a little, if he could have brought himself to realise them, in their narrow conventionality. Fortunately it did not occur to Mrs. Romayne to ask for them. With the ready tact of a woman of the world she turned the conversation with a gracefully worded question as to his recent expedition. He answered it with the courteous generality—only rather more gravely spoken—with which he had answered a great many similar questions put to him during the past week by ladies to whom he had been introduced in his capacity of momentary celebrity; and she passed on from one point to another with the superficial interest evoked by one of the topics of the hour. Her exaggerated comments and questions, more or less wide of the mark, were exhausted at length, and a moment's pause followed; a fact that indicated, though Falconer did not know it, that the preceding conversation had involved some kind of strain on the bright little woman who had kept it up so vivaciously. The pause was broken by Falconer.

"You have heard," he said, "of poor Thomson's illness?"

It would hardly be true to say that Mrs. Romayne started—even slightly—but a curious kind of flush seemed to pass across her face. As she answered, both her voice and her manner seemed instinctively to increase and emphasize that distance which she had tacitly set between them; it was as though the introduction into the conversation of a name their mutual familiarity with which represented mutual interests and connections had created the instinct in her.

"Yes, poor man!" she said carelessly. "There has been a good deal of illness about this season, somehow."

"I am afraid it is a bad business," went on Falconer, with no comprehension of the turn she had given to the conversation, and with his mental condemnation of what seemed to him simple heartlessness on her part not wholly absent from his voice. "There was to be a consultation to-day; and I shall call this evening to hear the result. But I am afraid there is very slender hope."

"How very sad!" said Mrs. Romayne with polite interest.

Falconer bent his head in grave assent, and then with a view to arousing in her shallow nature—as it seemed to him—some remembrance at least of the usefulness to her of the man whose probable death she contemplated so carelessly, he said with formal courtesy:

"Thomson has done all the work connected with our joint trusteeship so admirably hitherto that there has been no need for my services. But if, while he is ill, you should find yourself in want of his aid in that capacity, I need not say that I am entirely at your command."

Again that curious flush passed across Mrs. Romayne's face, leaving it rather pale this time.

"Thanks, so much!" she said quickly. "I really could not think of troubling you. I've no doubt I shall be able to hold on until Mr. Thomson is well again. Thanks immensely! You will not be within reach for very long, I suppose?"

"I shall be in London for a year, certainly," answered Falconer, acknowledging her tacit refusal to recognise any claim on him in the formal directness of his reply. Then, as she uttered a sharp little exclamation of surprise, he added briefly; "I am in the doctors' hands, unfortunately. There is something wrong with me, they say."

"I am very sorry——" she began prettily, though her eyes were rather hard and preoccupied. But at that moment the door opened to admit an influx of visitors, and Falconer rose to go.

"So glad to have seen you!" she said as she turned to him after welcoming the new-comers. "You won't have a cup of tea? It is always rather crushing when a man refuses one's tea, isn't it, Mrs. Anson?" turning as she spoke to a lady sitting close by. Then as she gave him her hand, speaking in a tone which still included the other lady in the conversation, she alluded for the first time to Julian. The whole call had gone by without one of those references to "my boy" with which all Mrs. Romayne's acquaintances were so familiar, that such an omission under the circumstances would have been hardly credible to any one of them.

"I'm so sorry you have missed my boy!" she said now with her apologetic laugh. "I'm afraid I am absurdly proud of him—isn't that so, dear Mrs. Anson?—but he really is a dear fellow."

"He is going to the bar, I believe?" said Falconer; his face and voice alike were uncompromisingly stern and unbending.

"Yes!" answered Julian's mother. "He is not clever, dear boy, but I hope he may do fairly well. Good-bye! Shall you be at the Gordons' to-night? We are going first to see the American actor they rave about so. A funny little domestic party—I and my son and my son's new and particular 'chum.' Good-bye!"

Mrs. Romayne's face did not regain its normal colour as she turned her attention to her other callers, nor did those faint lines about her mouth and eyes disappear. She was particularly charming that afternoon, but always, as she welcomed one set of visitors or parted from another, laughing, talking or listening so gaily, there was a faint, hardly definable air of preoccupation about her. She had a great many visitors, and the afternoon grew hotter as it wore on. When she dressed for dinner that night, finding herself strangely nervous, irritable with her maid, and "on edge altogether," as she expressed it, she was very definite and distinct in her self-assurances that such an unusual state of things was owing solely to the heat and "those tiresome people"; rather unnecessarily distinct and explicit it would have seemed, since there was apparently no chance of contradiction.

The acquaintanceship between Julian and Marston Loring had developed during the past fortnight with surprising rapidity. They had dined together at the club, they had smoked together in Loring's chambers, and they had met incessantly at dances, "at homes," or dinners, on all of which occasions Mrs. Romayne had been uniformly gracious to her son's friend.

At a garden-party a few miles out of London, admittedly the greatest failure of the season, when Loring and the Romaynes had walked about together all the afternoon with that carelessness of social obligations which a dull party is apt to engender, the scheme for the present evening had been arranged; Loring adding a preliminary dinner at a restaurant, with himself in the capacity of host to Mrs. Romayne and her son, to the original suggestion that they should go together to the theatre.

Julian was in high spirits as they drove off to keep their engagement, but his mother's responses to his chatter were neither so ready nor so bright as usual. He glanced at her once or twice and then said boyishly:

"You look awfully done up, mother!"

Mrs. Romayne turned to him quickly, her eyes sparkling angrily, her whole face looking irritable and annoyed.

"My dear Julian," she said sharply, "it's a very bad habit to be constantly commenting on people's appearance; especially when your remarks are uncomplimentary. You told me I looked tired the other day. Please don't do it again!"

Such an ebullition of temper was an almost unheard-of thing with Mrs. Romayne, and Julian could only stare at her in helpless astonishment—not hurt, but simply surprised, and inclined to be resentful. He could not realise as a woman might have done the jarred, quivering state of nerves implied in such an outbreak; and he simply thought his mother was rather odd, when a moment later she stretched out her hand hastily, and laid it on his with a quick, tight squeeze.

"That was abominably cross, dear!" she said in a voice which shook. "Don't mind! I am all right now."

But she was not all right, and though she made a valiant effort to collect her forces and appear so, her gaiety throughout dinner was strained and forced. Loring's quick perception realised instantly that something was wrong with her, and his demeanour under the circumstances was significant at once of the work of the past fortnight, and of his individual capacity for turning everything to his own ends. With a tacit assumption of a certain right to consider her, he evinced just such a delicate appreciation of her mood as gave her a sense of rest and soothing, without letting her feel for a moment that he found anything wanting in her. His pose was always that of a man to whom youth or even early manhood, with its follies and inexperiences, is a thing of the dim past, and he used that pose now to the utmost advantage; combining a mental equality with the mother with an actual equality with the son as his contemporary in a manner which made him seem in a very subtle way equally the friend of each. He talked, of course, almost exclusively to Mrs. Romayne, never, however, failing to include Julian in the conversation; and he so managed the conversation as to take all its trouble on his own shoulders, and give Mrs. Romayne little to do but listen and be entertained.

He succeeded so well that the dinner-hour, by the time it was over, had done the work of many days in advancing his dawning intimacy with Mrs. Romayne.

She felt better, she told herself as they entered the theatre—told herself with rather excessive eagerness and satisfaction, perhaps because of something within, of which the quick, nervous movement of her hands as she unfastened her cloak was the outward and visible sign.

The curtain was just going up as they seated themselves, and during the first quarter of an hour the two seats to their left remained empty. Then Mrs. Romayne, whose attention was by no means chained to the stage, became aware of the slow and difficult approach of a flow of loudly-whispered and apologetic conversation, combined with the large person of a lady; and a moment or two later she was being fallen over by Mrs. Halse, who was followed by a girl, and who continued to explain the situation fluently and audibly, until a distinct expression of the opinion of the pit caused her to subside temporarily.

She began to talk again before the applause on the fall of the curtain had died away, and her voice reached Mrs. Romayne, to whom her remarks were addressed, across the girl who was with her, and Julian, who was sitting on his mother's left hand, with gradually increasing distinctness.

"So curious that our seats should be together!" were the first words Mrs. Romayne heard. "I have just been meeting a connection of yours. The explorer, you know—Dennis Falconer. So fascinating! Oh, by-the-bye—my cousin. I don't think she has had the pleasure of being introduced to you, though she has met your son. Miss Hilda Newton—Mrs. Romayne."

Miss Hilda Newton was a very pretty, dark girl of a somewhat pronounced type. She had large, perceptive, black eyes, singularly unabashed; a charming little turned-up nose; and a rather large mouth with a good deal of shrewd character about it. She was understood to be a country cousin of Mrs. Halse's, with whom she had been staying for the last three weeks; but only a very critical and rather unkind eye could have traced the country cousin in her dress, which had a great deal of style and dash about it. She acknowledged Mrs. Halse's introduction of her with rather excessive self-possession, and after a casual word or two to Mrs. Romayne, addressed herself to Julian; it was she with whom he had disappeared to supper at Lady Bracondale's "at home," and they had evidently seen a good deal of one another in the interval.

Mrs. Romayne had noticed them together more than once, and she had taken a dislike to Miss Newton's pretty, independent face and manners. In her present mood it was an absolute relief to her to find in the girl a legitimate excuse for irritation, and a reason for the fact that Mrs. Halse's speech had somehow undone all the work of the early part of the evening, and set her nerves on edge afresh.

"Detestably bad style!" she said to herself angrily, giving an unheeding ear to Mrs. Halse as she watched Miss Newton reply with a little twirl of her fan to an eager question of Julian's. "Just what one would expect in a cousin of that woman." Then she became aware that "that woman" was vociferously insisting on changing places with Julian, and that Julian was acceding to the proposition with considerable alacrity; and before she had well realised exactly what the change involved, Mrs. Halse, with much paraphernalia of smelling-bottle, fan, opera-glasses, and programme, was established at her side, and Julian and Miss Newton were seated together at the end of the row, practically isolated by the stream of Mrs. Halse's conversation.

"So horrid to talk across people, isn't it?" said that lady airily, though no crowd ever collected would have interfered with her flow of language. "This is much more comfortable. My dear Mrs. Romayne, I am simply dying to rave to somebody about your cousin—he is your cousin, isn't he?—Mr. Falconer, you know. What a splendid man! Of course all the accounts of his work have been most fascinating, but the man himself makes it all seem so much more real, don't you know. Now, do tell me, is he your first cousin, and do you remember him when he was quite a little boy, and all that sort of thing?"

Mrs. Romayne took up her fan and unfurled it. She was looking past Mrs. Halse at Julian and Miss Newton, who were looking over the same programme with their heads rather close together. Her eyebrows were slightly contracted, and her eyes very bright, and the restless movements of the slender hand that held the fan seemed to be an expression of intense inward irritation.

"Oh dear, no; Dennis Falconer is not my first cousin, by any means!" she said carelessly, though her voice was a trifle sharp. "Third or fourth, or something of that kind."

"He is quite a hero, isn't he?" said Mrs. Halse, gushingly addressing Loring. "Have you met him?"

Loring, though his glance had every appearance of perfect carelessness, was watching Mrs. Romayne intently. He had noticed her access of nervous irritability, and he was curious as to the cause. Was it her son's flirtation with Miss Newton? Was it dislike to Mrs. Halse? Or had it any connection with Dennis Falconer? He had his reasons for a study of Mrs. Romayne's idiosyncrasies.

"Yes," he said. "I met him the other night. A good sort of fellow he seemed."

"He's magnificent!" said Mrs. Halse enthusiastically. "We must have him at the bazaar, my dear Mrs. Romayne; that I am quite determined. If he would sell African trophies for us, you know—a native's tooth, or poppy-heads—oh, arrow-heads, is it?—well anything of that sort—it would be a fortune to us! Have you seen a great deal of him? Cousins are so often just like brothers and sisters, are they not?"

A low laugh and a toss of her head from Miss Newton at this moment closed the perusal of the programme, and Julian turned his attention to perusing the pretty black eyes instead. Mrs. Romayne's lips seemed to tighten and whiten, and the fingers which held the fan were tightly clenched as she answered in a voice which rang hard in spite of her efforts:

"Sometimes they are, of course. But it depends so much on circumstances. Dennis Falconer and I had not met for years until the other day."

At that moment the curtain went up, leaving Mrs. Halse literally with her mouth open, and the instant it fell Mrs. Romayne leant across to Miss Newton with a comment on the performance, spoken in a rather thin, tense voice, and with eyes that glittered as though the nervous strain under which the speaker was labouring was becoming almost insupportable. Apparently something in her face repelled the girl, for her answer was of the briefest, and Julian throwing himself into the breach, he and Miss Newton were instantly absorbed in an animated discussion. It was a long wait, and Loring, noting every one of the restless movements of the woman by his side as she talked and laughed so sharply, understood that to Mrs. Romayne every moment meant nervous torture. The instant the green curtain fell on the third act she rose, and Loring followed her example, and wrapped her quickly and deftly in her cloak.

"I can't say I think much of your American prodigy," she said to him with a forced laugh. "I must confess that he has bored me to such an extent that I really can't stand any more boredom, and shall go straight home. Julian!"

She glanced round for him as she spoke, but he was escorting Mrs. Halse and her cousin, and she was waiting for him in her brougham before he joined her.

"Suppose you come to the club with me?" suggested Loring carelessly, as Julian received his mother's announcement of her intentions rather blankly. "What do you say to a game of billiards?"

"All right," responded Julian. "Thanks, old fellow. It was only that I told Miss Newton we were coming on. Isn't she a jolly girl, mother?"

Mrs. Romayne smiled.

"Very pretty indeed," she said lightly. "It's a sad pity you're such an ineligible fellow, isn't it?"

And Loring, as the carriage drove off, said to himself admiringly: "What a wonderfully clever woman!"

Reaction from a heavy strain—even, apparently, if it is only the strain of combating exhaustion engendered by heat—is a terrible thing. When Mrs. Romayne got out of her carriage after her long drive, her face was haggard and drawn. She passed into the house, gathered up mechanically, and without a glance, two letters waiting for her on the hall-table; told the maid who was waiting for her that she might go to bed, and went up into the drawing-room.

There was a low chair by a little table covered with dainty, useless paraphernalia, which she particularly affected. She sat down in it now, almost unconsciously as it seemed, without even loosening her cloak, and with a long, low sigh; the moments passed, and still she sat there, a curious grey pallor about her face, her eyes gazing straight before her as though they were looking into the future or the past. At last, as if by a sudden fierce effort of will, she roused herself and began to tear open the letters still in her hand as if with a desperate instinct towards occupying her thoughts.

Her eyes fell on the letter by this time open in her hand, and she read it almost unconsciously, taking in the sense gradually as she read:

"Dear Cousin Hermia,

"I have just heard to my great sorrow of the death of our old friend Thomson, and I think it right to let you know of it. I believe I need not remind you that on any future occasion on which the help of your now, unfortunately, sole trustee may be necessary, you will find me entirely at your service.

"Faithfully yours,
"Dennis Falconer."

With a sudden fierce gesture, of which her small white fingers looked hardly capable, Mrs. Romayne crushed the letter in her hand and lifted her head.

"To be thrown upon him!" she said in a curious, breathless tone. "To have to come into contact—close contact, personal contact—with him!"

CHAPTER XII

THE season, as Mrs. Romayne had told Dennis Falconer, was to be a short one, and its proceedings were apparently to be regulated on the old principle of a short life and a merry one. Gaieties overtook one another in too rapid succession, and an unusually sunny and breezy May and June, with the inevitable action of such weather on human beings, even under the most artificial conditions, rendered these gaieties a shade more really gay than usual.

The atmosphere was not, again, so close as it had been on the afternoon when Dennis Falconer called on Mrs. Romayne, and it is presumable that the weather must have been responsible for her general unusualness of mood on the evening of that day; for if she was not quite herself on the following morning, the touch of self-compulsion in her brightness was so slight as to be hardly perceptible, and a day or two later it had entirely disappeared.

Certainly if constant stir and movement are conducive to good spirits, there was nothing wonderful in Mrs. Romayne's satisfaction with life. For she had not, as she complained laughingly, a single moment to herself.

"It's a regular treadmill!" she exclaimed gaily one day to Lord Garstin. "I had really forgotten what a terrible thing a London season was!"

"It seems to agree with you," was the answer. "There is one lady of my acquaintance, and only one, who seems to grow younger every day!"

"You can't mean me," she laughed. "I assure you, I am growing grey with incessantly running after that boy of mine! He is as difficult to catch as any lion of the season. I never see him except at parties!"

Julian's intimacy with Marston Loring had grown apace, and it had led to sundry social consequences which were, his mother said, "so good for him." Little dinners at the club, to which he had been duly elected; dinners at which he was now guest, now host; jovial little bachelor suppers made up among the very best "sets." Loring himself was very careful—though he knew better than to make his care perceptible, except in its results—never to allow himself to be placed in the position of a rival to Mrs. Romayne for her son's time and company. He lost no opportunity of making himself useful and agreeable to Mrs. Romayne; now using pleasantly arrogated rights as Julian's friend; now his superior brain-power and knowledge of the world; until he gradually assumed the position of friend of the house. But club life necessarily created in Julian interests apart from his mother—interests which she was apparently well content that he should have, so long as his ever-ready chatter to her on the subject revealed that they were all connected with good "sets."

It was furthermore a season of very pretty *débutantes*, a large majority of whom elected to look upon Mr. Romayne as "such a nice boy," and to exact—or permit—any amount of slavery from him in the matters of fetching and carrying and general attendance. "You're known to be so profoundly ineligible, you see!" his mother would say to him, laughing. "Nobody is in the least afraid of you, poor boy!" And she looked on with perfect calmness as he danced, and rode, and did church parade; looked on with a calmness which might have been mistaken for indifference, but for the significant fact that she always knew which of his "jolly girls" was in the ascendant for the moment.

Miss Newton had gone home on the day following the meeting at the theatre.

Falconer was to be seen about throughout the season, making his grave concession to the weaknesses of society. Mrs. Romayne and Julian met him constantly, and he was asked to, and attended, the most formal of the dinners given at Queen Anne Street. But the intercourse between him and his "connection," as Mrs. Romayne called herself, was of the most distant and non-progressive type. Julian did not take to him at all. "He is such a solemn fellow, mother!" he said. "He seems to think that I'm doing something wrong all the time." An observation to which Mrs. Romayne replied by laughing a rather forced laugh and changing the conversation.

The last event of the season, as it became evident as the weeks ran on, would be the bazaar in aid of Mrs. Halse's discovery among charities. It was, perhaps, as well that the institution in question was by no means in such urgent need of patronage as might have been argued from Mrs. Halse's demeanour towards it earlier in the proceedings; for that lady's enthusiasm on the subject had suffered severely in the contest with the numerous other enthusiasms which had succeeded it, and the affairs of the bazaar had been pursued by all its supporters with energy which is most charitably to be described as intermittent. Three separate dates had been fixed for the opening day; and, after a great deal of money had been spent in printing and advertising, each of these in succession had had to be abandoned owing to the singular incompleteness of every fundamental arrangement—though, as Mrs. Halse observed impatiently, after the third postponement, there were "heaps and heaps of Chinese lanterns." Finally it was announced for the fifth and sixth of July; and owing to herculean efforts on the part of half-a-dozen unfortunate men enlisted in the cause; who apparently braced themselves to the task with a desperate sense that if the affair was not somehow or another carried through now, by fair means or foul, they were doomed to struggle in a tumultuous sea of fashionable feminine futility for the remainder of their miserable lives; on the fifth the bazaar was actually opened.

It was late in the evening of that eventful day, and in various fashionable drawing-rooms exhausted ladies stretched on sofas were recruiting their forces after their severe labours. It had been the fashion for the last week or more among the prospective stall-holders to allude to the fatigue before them with resigned and heroic sighs of awful import; consequently they were now convinced to a woman that they were in the last stages of exhaustion. As a matter of fact it is doubtful whether out of the sensations of all the "smart" helpers concerned—with the exception of the devoted half-dozen before mentioned, who had retired to various clubs in a state of collapse—a decent state of fatigue could have been constructed; and the reason for this was threefold. In the first place, so much money had been spent in announcing the dates when the bazaar did not take place, that there was exceedingly little forthcoming to announce the date when it did take place; consequently its attractive existence remained almost unknown to the general public, and the services of the sellers were in very slight demand. In the second place, the greater part of the work which could not be done by proxy was left undone. And in the third place, each lady had been throughout the day so deeply convinced of the "frightfully tiring" nature of her occupation, that she thought it only her duty to "save herself" whenever that course was open to her—which was almost always.

In the drawing-room at Chelsea, very cool and pretty with its open windows and its plentiful supply of flowers and ferns, Mrs. Romayne was lying on the sofa, as the exigencies of the moment, socially speaking, demanded of her, in an attitude of graceful weariness; an attitude which was rather belied by the alert expression of her contented face. She had dined at home—"just a quiet little dinner, you know—cold, because goodness knows when we shall get it!"—with Julian and Loring at half-past seven. The bazaar did not close until nine, but all the principal stall-holders had thought it their duty to the following day not to wear themselves quite out, and had left the last two hours to the care of one or other of the hangers-on, of whom "smart" women may usually have a supply if they choose; and Mrs. Romayne's quiet little dinner was only one of a score of similar functions, very dainty and luxurious in view of the tremendous exertions which had preceded them, which were being held in various fashionable parts of London. At ten o'clock Loring had taken his leave, declaring sympathetically that Mrs. Romayne must long for perfect quiet after her exertions. It was then that Mrs. Romayne had betaken herself to her sofa and her papers.

"What an immense time it is since we have had such a domesticated hour!"

Mrs. Romayne had laid down her literature some moments before, and had been lying looking at Julian with that curious expression in her eyes which would creep into them now and again when they rested on the good-looking young figure, and which harmonised so ill with the shallow, vivacious prettiness of the rest of her face. She spoke, however, with her usual light laugh at herself, and Julian laughed too as he threw down his magazine and turned towards her.

"It is an age, isn't it?" he said.

During the final agony of preparation for the bazaar, Julian had been in immense request. Not that he was one of the devoted half-dozen, or that he did much definite work; but he was always ready to discuss any lady's private fad with her for any length of time, and to rush all over London about nothing. His exertions, and the exhaustion engendered thereby, had rendered necessary a great deal of recreation at the club. He had repaired thither very frequently of late, instead of escorting his mother home on the conclusion of their tale of parties for the night.

"It is a comfort to think that it is so nearly over!" observed Mrs. Romayne carelessly. It is never worth while, in the world in which Mrs. Romayne moved, to express more than half your meaning in words, and Julian quite understood that she alluded, not to the domestic hour, but to the season. Her words were not prompted by any actual weariness of the round of life she characterised as "it," but the sentiment was in the air—the fashionable air, that is to say. She and Julian, in common with the greater part of their world, were leaving London at the end of the week.

"It has been awfully jolly!" said Julian, leaning back in his chair and resting his head against his loosely locked hands. "I had no idea that life was such a first-rate business!"

His mother smiled, and there was a strange touch of triumph in her smile.

"It is a first-rate business," she assented, "if one lives it among the right people and in the right position. I imagine you see by this time that it isn't much use otherwise!"

He laughed as though his appreciation of her words rendered them almost a truism to him, and there was a moment's silence. It was broken by Julian.

"It costs a lot of money," he said, in a casual, indefinite way, but with a quick glance at his mother.

"Well, it isn't cheap, certainly," was the laughing answer: "but I think we shall manage." Then noticing something a little deprecating about his pose and expression, Mrs. Romayne added, with mock reprehension, "You're not going to ask me to raise your allowance, you extravagant boy?"

Julian moved, and leaning forward, clasped his hands round one knee as if the uncomfortable and transitory pose assisted explanation. He laughed back at her, but he was looking nevertheless somewhat ashamed of himself.

"No, it's not that—exactly," he began rather lamely. "It's a splendid allowance, mother dear, and I'm no end grateful; but the fact is, there has been a good deal of card-playing lately at the club. I don't care for cards, you know, but one must play a bit, and I have been rather a fool. Look here, dear, I suppose—I suppose you couldn't let me have two hundred, could you—before we go away, you know?"

"Two hundred, Julian! My dear boy!"

There was a strong tone of surprise and remonstrance in Mrs. Romayne's voice, and there was also a very distinct note of annoyance; but all these sentiments seemed rather to apply to the demand, which was apparently unseasonable, than to the desirability of the transaction. She was neither startled nor distressed.

"It is young Fordyce, mother," continued her son deprecatingly. "It was awfully foolish to play with him, he's so beastly lucky. And you see I must settle it before I go away."

"And have you none of your own?" demanded his mother, with some asperity in her tone. Julian's creditor was a young man who had the reputation of being a "very good sort of fellow," who would never "do" in society.

"I'm awfully sorry to say I haven't!" returned Julian meekly.

There was a moment's pause, and Mrs. Romayne tapped impatiently on the papers lying by her.

"It is such an inconvenient moment," she said at last. "I have just made all my arrangements for the quarter—I don't mean that you can't have it, of course you can, dear—but it is difficult to lay my hand on it at this moment."

"Falconer could arrange it for you," suggested Julian, alluding to Falconer in his capacity of trustee for the first time, as it happened.

Mrs. Romayne started violently, and a sharp exclamation of dissent rose to her lips. She stopped it half uttered, and paused a moment, controlling herself with difficulty.

"No," she said at last, in rather a hard tone. "I would rather not do that. I will think it over and see what can be done. We must raise your allowance, sir. I can't have mines sprung on me like this!"

She had risen as she spoke, and as he followed her example she lifted her face towards him for the good-night kiss which always passed between them.

"I will sleep upon it," she said. "Good night, extravagant boy."

CHAPTER XIII

THE stall-holders presented a singularly fresh and unworn appearance, considering how much they had undergone, as they gradually put in an appearance at their stall on the following day, and gathered together in little knots to compare notes as to their sufferings, and here and there to allude incidentally to their takings—which certainly seemed disproportionate to the exertions of which they were the result. The fancy dress idea on which Mrs. Halse's whole soul had been set in March had been abandoned when Mrs. Halse found a fresh hobby in April; and each lady wore that variety of the fashion of the day which seemed most desirable in her eyes. All the dresses were very "smart," and as their wearers moved about, visiting one another's stalls, exchanging greetings, and inspecting one another's wares with critical eyes, they showed to conspicuous advantage. For, during the first hour at least, the stall-holders and their satellites, male and female—a mere handful of people in the great hall—had the entire place with all its decorations to themselves.

It was the cheap day, however, and as the afternoon wore on the hall gradually filled with that curious class of person which is always craving for any link, however "sham," with the fashionable world, and makes it a point of self-respect to attend all public functions in which "society" chances to be engaged. These far-off votaries of fashion walked about, looking not at the stalls, but at the ladies in attendance on them, turning away as a rule in stolid silence when invited in mellifluous tones to buy; or perhaps investing a shilling when long search had resulted in the discovery of a twopenny article to be had for that sum, for the sake of making a purchase from one of the leaders of fashion; some of them, with a vague notion that it was fashionable to "know every one," kept up a great show of talk and laughter, and were constantly seeing acquaintances on the other side of the hall—with whom they never by any chance came in contact. But no one spent more than five shillings, and the stall-holders began to find the position pall.

"I call this deadly!" said Mrs. Halse, subsiding into a chair, and looking up pathetically at Julian Romayne, who stood by. Julian should have been in attendance at the stall next but one, where Mrs. Pomeroy and his mother reigned, but Mrs. Halse, in view of the exertions before her, had summoned to her aid, about a week before, Miss Hilda Newton; and Miss Hilda Newton was looking irresistibly bewitching to-day in a big yellow hat. Her spirits, also, bore the strain of the proceedings better than did those of the other young ladies.

"Suppose we pick out some things—cheap things"—with a little grimace—"and go about among the people and try and sell them," she said now adventurously, looking up into Julian's face, with her pretty black eyes dancing. "I've done it heaps of times at bazaars, and it always goes well. Let us try, Mr. Romayne."

Mr. Romayne was by no means loath, and a few minutes later his mother, whose eyes had been covering Mrs. Halse's stall all the time she tried to persuade into a purchase a sharp-faced girl, whose sole object was a sufficiently prolonged inspection of Mrs. Romayne's dress to enable her to find out how "that body was made," saw them sally forth together laughing and talking in low, confidential tones. Her lips tightened slightly; the reappearance of Miss Newton had found Mrs. Romayne's dislike to the pretty, opinionated, self-reliant girl as active and apparently unreasoning as it had been on her previous visit.

"What a very good idea!" she said now suavely, turning to Mrs. Pomeroy who sat by, a picture of placid content, and indicating the adventurous pair as they disappeared among the people. "We must try something of the sort, I think. Maud, dear"—Miss Pomeroy had recently become Maud to Mrs. Romayne—"do you see? I really think something might be done in that way."

Miss Pomeroy, who was standing in front of the stall, a charming and apparently quite inanimate figure in white, assented demurely, and Mrs. Romayne, looking round for a man, caught the eye of Loring. He came to her instantly.

"You'll do capitally," she said brightly, and Miss Pomeroy, making no objection to the proceeding, was started forth with Loring, the latter carrying a small stock-in-trade, to emulate Miss Newton and Julian. That stock-in-trade was quite untouched, however, when about a quarter of an hour later they returned to the stall a little hot and discomfited.

"We haven't made a success," said Loring with a rather sardonic smile; "Miss Pomeroy says I'm no good! Now, there's that fellow Julian doing a roaring trade!"

Julian and Miss Newton, in point of fact, were at that moment visible returning to Mrs. Halse's stall, evidently in high feather, all their stock sold out. Mrs. Romayne watched Julian counting his gains into Mrs. Halse's hand, saying laughingly to Loring as she did so:

"You are not boy enough for this kind of thing, I'm afraid!" And then Julian, with a final laughing nod, turned away from Mrs. Halse, and came hastily towards his mother's stall.

"That's right!" said Mrs. Romayne gaily, ignoring the fact that he had evidently not come to stay. "I was just wanting you, sir, to go round with

Miss Pomeroy, if she will kindly go with you, and get rid of some of our odds and ends!"

Julian stopped short and flushed a little.

"I'm awfully sorry!" he said. "I'll come back and do it with pleasure! But I have just promised to go round again with Miss Newton. I came to see if you could give us some change."

His mother supplied his wants smilingly, and he was gone. She had turned away with rather compressed lips when a voice behind her said half hesitatingly, half gushingly, and with a strong German accent:

"We are surely unmistaken! It is—yes, it must be, the much-honoured Mrs. Romayne!"

Mrs. Romayne turned quickly and gazed at the speaker obviously unrecognisingly. Nor did the two figures with whom she was confronted look in the least like acquaintances of hers. They were young women of the plainest and most angular German type, shabbily dressed according to the canons of middle-class German taste.

"She remembers us not, Gretchen!" began the younger of the two. And then a sudden light of recollection broke over Mrs. Romayne. They were two girls who had been training for a musical career at Leipsic, whom it had been the fashion to patronise; they had not developed as had been expected, however, and she had entirely forgotten their existence.

"Fräulein Schmitz!" she said now with distant brightness. "Ah, of course! How stupid of me! How do you do?"

They were very loquacious. Mrs. Romayne had heard all about their careers; all the reasons that had led to their spending a fortnight in London; and was beginning to think that the moment had come for getting rid of them, when, having exhausted themselves in compliments on her appearance, they enquired after Julian.

"Though we have seen Mr. Romayne," said the elder, "since, ah, but much since we had the pleasure to see his mother. It was in Alexandria in the winter past—we hoped that some concerts there might be possible, but there is so much jealousy and favouritism—it was in Alexandria that we met him. He was travelling in Egypt, he told to us."

"Yes!" said Mrs. Romayne, smothering a yawn. "He was in Egypt——" she stopped suddenly, and her eyes seemed to contract strangely. "Where did you say you saw him?" she said.

"It was in Alexandria! He was there for the day only, and he was to us most kind. He arrived in the morning early by the same train, and he showed us much until at night he left."

"At Alexandria?"

"Surely! At Alexandria!"

"You must have made a mistake. It was some other place."

Mrs. Romayne's tone was curiously unlike that in which she had conducted the early part of the conversation. It was sharp and direct. Fräulein Schmitz seemed to notice and resent the change.

"But we have not made a mistake, I must assure you!" she said stiffly. "It was at Alexandria. We saw him go away in the train."

There was a moment's pause. Mrs. Romayne was looking straight before her with those strangely contracted eyes; her lips a thin, pale line. The sisters waited a moment, evidently affronted. Then, finding that Mrs. Romayne took no notice whatever of them, they exchanged resentful glances, and the elder spoke.

"We will say good-bye!" she said formally. "It is time that we were going!"

Mrs. Romayne seemed to remember their presence—gradually only. Then she said quickly, and in a voice that sounded as though her throat were dry:

"You are going at once? Right out of the hall at once?"

"At once we are going, yes!" was the reply, and with a stiff inclination of their heads they moved away.

Mrs. Romayne followed the two angular forms with her eyes until they reached the entrance and disappeared. Then she swept a quick glance round the hall. Julian was at the further end deeply absorbed in his proceedings with Miss Newton. The Fräulein Schmitz had evidently been unseen by him.

His mother looked at him for a moment with a strange, fixed gaze, and then she turned her eyes away mechanically, and moved her mouth with a little twitch as though she felt the muscles stiffening and knew that they must not take the lines they would; there was a deadly pallor about her mouth. At that instant Loring came up to her with a witty satirical comment on the scene at which she was apparently gazing, and for the next few minutes she stood there exchanging gay little observations with him, the pallor never altering, her eyes never moving. Then quite suddenly she turned towards him.

"I want some tea!" she said. "Take me to the refreshment place, Mr. Loring!"

Julian was threading his way to where she stood, and though she turned instantly in the direction of the refreshment stall, followed perforce by Loring, she passed close to him. He stopped and said something, but she only nodded to him and went rapidly on.

A great many other stall-holders were recruiting themselves with tea and ices, and they were all more or less in spirits, real or affected, at the approaching prospect of the end of their labours. Mrs. Romayne was instantly hailed as one of a very smart group, and took her place with eager, high-pitched gaiety. She did not go back to her stall, tea being over, but moved about the bazaar, always with a little party in attendance, laughing and talking. She and Julian were dining with a large party of stall-holders at Mrs. Pomeroy's; they were all to repair thither direct from the bazaar, and Mrs. Romayne took a detachment in her carriage. Only one instant of solitude came to her before the luxurious, hilarious meal; only one instant, when the stream of descending ladies left her behind on an upper landing. In that instant, as if involuntarily and unconsciously to herself, the gaiety fell from her face like a mask, leaving it haggard and ghastly. She put her hand—it was icy cold—up to her head.

"He told me a lie!" she said to herself. "A lie! Oh, my boy!"

She was very bright and witty as she and Julian drove home together, and the greyish whiteness which was stealing over her face was unnoticed by her son's careless eyes even when they stood in the well-lighted hall.

"Are you going straight up, mother?" he said. "If so, I'll say good night. I want a cigar."

She paused a moment and looked at him with that indescribable tenderness which haunted her eyes at times as they rested on him, intensified a thousandfold.

"I'll come and sit with you for a little while if you will have me," she said.

She tried evidently for her usual manner, and succeeded inasmuch as Julian noticed nothing beyond. But beneath the surface there was something not wholly to be suppressed—something which looked out of her eyes, trembled in her voice, lingered in her touch as she laid her hand on his arm; something which, taken in conjunction with the shreds of affectation with which she strove to cover it, and with the boy's profound unconsciousness, was as pathetic as it was beautiful and strange.

She drew him into his own little room, and then with a forced laugh at herself she pushed him gently into a chair, and insisted on waiting upon him— bringing him cigar, matches, ash-tray—anything she could think of to add to his comfort, laughing all the time at him and at herself, and hugging those shreds of affectation close. But there was that about her, if there had been any one to see and understand, which made her one with all the many mothers since the world began who, with their hearts aching and bleeding with impotent pity and love, have tried to find some outlet for their yearning in the strange instinct for service which goes always hand in hand with mother love as with no other love on earth.

She lit his match at last, and then knelt down beside his chair.

"My dearest," she said, "my dearest, you shall have that two hundred—to-morrow if you like! You did not think me vexed about it, did you? You know I only want you to be happy, Julian, don't you?"

Julian laid down his cigar with a merry laugh. "I should be a fool if I didn't!" he answered, patting her hand with boyish affection. "It's awfully good of you, dear, and I'm frightfully grateful. I won't make such a fool of myself again."

Mrs. Romayne put up her hand quickly. "Don't promise, Julian!" she said in a strange breathless way, "you might—you might forget, you know, and then perhaps you wouldn't like to tell me! And I want to know! I always want to know!" She stopped abruptly, an almost agonised appeal in her eyes.

She was still kneeling at his side, with her eyes fixed on his face; and suddenly, abruptly, almost as though the words forced themselves from her against her will, she said, with a slight catch in her voice:

"Julian, I met Fräulein Schmitz to-day!"

He met her eyes for a moment, his own questioning and uncomprehending; then gradually there stole over his face recollection, vague at first, which became as it grew definite rather shamefaced, rather annoyed, and rather amused.

"Oh!" he said; his tone was light and daring enough, though a touch of genuine shame and embarrassment lurked in it. "Oh, I call that hard lines!"

He was smiling daringly into her face with an acceptance of the situation that was perfectly frank. His mother's hands, as they rested on the arm of his chair, were tightly wrung together, and her eyes never stirred from his face.

"Why?" she said rather hoarsely, "why did you?"

He laughed, shrugging his shoulders and throwing out his hands with a graceful foreign movement.

"I was rather a culprit, you see," he said. "I only spent those few hours in Alexandria, and I never gave a thought to your commission. And I felt such a brute about it that I wasn't up to confessing!"

It was the truth and the whole truth, and it conveyed itself as such. Mrs. Romayne knelt there for a moment more, looking into his eyes, her own wide and strained; and then she rose heavily and slowly to her feet. There was a pause.

The silence was broken by Julian, evidently with a view to changing a subject on which he could hardly be said to show to conspicuous advantage.

"You're going to write to Falconer, I suppose? You wouldn't like to do it to-night, dear, would you? He would get the letter in better time if it was posted the first thing. You could do it at my table there!"

Mrs. Romayne did not speak. Julian could not see her face.

"Yes!" she said at last, and her voice sounded rather hollow and far away, "I will do it to-night if you like." She bent down and kissed him. "Good night!" she said.

"Won't you write here?" said Julian in some surprise.

"No, I'll go upstairs!" she answered, and went out of the room.

She went upstairs, moving slowly and heavily, straight to her dainty little writing-table, and sat down, drawing out a sheet of paper. She wrote the conventional words of address to Dennis Falconer, and then she stopped suddenly and lifted her face. It was ghastly. The eyes, sunken and dim, seemed to be confronting the very irony of fate.

CHAPTER XIV

"THE jolliest week I've ever had in my life!"

"I wonder how often you've said that before?"

August had come and gone, the greater part of September had followed in its wake, and a ruddy September sun was making the end of the summer glorious. In the large garden of a large country house in Norfolk, everything seen in its wonderful radiance seemed to be even overcharged with colour, if such a thing is possible with nature; it was as though all the beauty of the summer had been intensified and arrested in its maturity into one final glow. The rich green of the smooth lawns, the colours of the autumnal flowers, the tints of the foliage, the very atmosphere, seemed all alike to be pausing for the moment at the most perfect point of radiance. But nature never pauses; and that this was indeed the final glow, the end of her summer beauty, was revealed here and there by little significant touches, or written across earth and sky in broader letters. The birds were gone or going. Even as Julian Romayne spoke a flight of swallows overhead was wheeling and darting hither and thither in preparation for an imminent departure; the very glory of the trees meant decay, and in spite of all the efforts of indefatigable gardeners, dead leaves strewed the trim lawns and gravel paths.

All these signs and tokens of the approach of the inevitable end were particularly conspicuous about the narrow grass path shut in by high yew hedges, up and down which Julian Romayne and Hilda Newton were sauntering together. Fallen leaves were thick upon it, and in the flower-beds, by which it was bordered, the summer flowers, whose day was long since done, had not been replaced by their autumn successors. Apparently, the walk was a secluded and little frequented one, on which it was not worth while to spend much pains. Judging from the coquettish toss of the head, tempered by a certain softness of tone, with which Miss Newton replied to the insinuated regret of Julian's words, it seemed not improbable that those characteristics had something to do with their selection of that particular spot for their stroll. They had been staying in this pleasant country house together for the last week, the hostess having taken a fancy to Mrs. Halse's cousin in town; and now in another hour Julian and his mother would be on their way home.

As the half-mocking, half-inviting words fell from his companion's lips, Julian turned impetuously towards the pretty, piquant face; it was shaded by a bewitching garden hat.

"I never meant it so much before, on my honour," he said impulsively; adding with a boyish suggestion of tender reproach in his voice: "I should have thought you might have known that. It's awfully hard lines to think it's over."

Miss Newton had a large crimson dahlia in her hand, and she was plucking the petals slowly away and scattering them at her feet.

"Is it?" she said.

"You know it is," he returned ardently, trying to catch a glimpse of the dark face bent over the crimson flower. "Won't you tell me that you're a little sorry, too? Miss Newton—Hilda——"

His vigorous young hand was just closing over the pretty little fingers that held the dahlia; the dainty little figure was yielding to him nothing loath, it seemed, when from the further end of the grass walk a third voice broke in upon their *tête-à-tête*, and as they started instinctively apart Mrs. Romayne, accompanied by their hostess, came sauntering towards them.

"Taking a farewell look at the quaint old walk, Julian?" she said with suave carelessness as she drew near them. "The garden is looking too beautiful this morning, isn't it, Miss Newton? What a lovely dahlia that is you were showing Julian!"

She looked smilingly at Miss Newton as she spoke, apparently quite unconscious that the girl's face was white—not with embarrassment, disappointment, or emotion, but with sheer angry resentment—and she moved on as she spoke, tacitly compelling Miss Newton to move on at her side, while Julian and the other lady followed, perforce together.

"We have only about ten minutes more, I'm afraid," she said. "I was just taking a last stroll round the place with Mrs. Ponsonby. I'm afraid we shall find London rather unbearable to-night. The call of duty is always so very inconvenient!"

She was leading the way toward the house, and her little high-pitched laugh eliciting only a monosyllabic response from the girl at her side, she resumed what was practically a monologue, carried on with a suavity and ease which was perhaps over-elaborated by just a touch. Her farewells, which followed almost immediately on their arrival at the house, when a little bustle of departure ensued—in which Miss Newton took no part, that young lady having promptly disappeared—were characterised by the same manner, about which there was also a little touch of suppressed excitement. It was not until she and Julian were alone together in a first-class carriage of the London express that her gay words and laughs ceased, and she let herself sink back in her corner, unfolding a newspaper with a short, hardly audible sigh of relief.

A very slight and indefinable change had come to Mrs. Romayne's face in the course of the last two months. It had been perceptible in her animation, and was still more perceptible in her repose. The lines about her face which had needed special influences to bring them into prominence during the winter were always plainly perceptible now; and they gave her face a very slightly careworn look, which was emphasized by the expression of her eyes and mouth.

The eyes had always a slightly restless look in them in these days; even now, as she read her paper, or appeared to read it, there was no concentration in them; and every now and then they were lifted hastily, almost furtively, over the paper's edge. The mouth was at once weaker and more determined; weaker, inasmuch as it had grown more sensitive, more nervously responsive to the movements of her restless eyes; and more determined, as though with the expression of a constant mental attitude.

There was a good deal of indecision in her face, and its expression varied slightly, but incessantly, as she fixed her eyes anew on the printed words before her after each fleeting glance at the boyish face outlined by the cushions opposite. She laid down her paper at last, with a little deliberate rustle, apparently intended to attract attention, and as she did so her face assumed its ordinary superficial vivacity; an expression which harmonised less well with the rather sharpened features than it had done three months before.

"A good novel, Julian?" she said airily, smothering a yawn as she spoke, and indicating with a little gesture of her head the book in Julian's hand.

Julian had been holding the book in his hand, ever since they left the little Norfolk station from which they had started, but he had scarcely turned a page. His features were composed into an expression of boyish resentment, about which there was that distinct suggestion of sullenness which is the usual outward expression of the hauteur of youth. As his mother spoke he flushed hotly with angry self-consciousness.

"Not particularly," he said, without lifting his eyes.

There was a moment's pause, during which Mrs. Romayne's eyes were fixed upon him with concentration enough in them now; and then she broke into a light laugh, and leaning suddenly forward laid one of her hands on his.

"Poor old boy!" she said, in a tone half mocking, half sympathising. "It was very hard on you, wasn't it? It's a cruel fate that makes young men so ineligible, and girls so pretty, and throws the two perversely together! If you've any thought to spare from yourself, sir, though, I think you should bestow a little gratitude upon me for my very timely arrival!"

She laughed again, and in her laugh, as in her voice, there was the faintest possible touch of reality, and that reality was anxiety. Then, as Julian twisted his hand from under hers with a gruff and almost inaudible: "I don't see that!" she leant back in her seat again with a smile.

"My dear boy," she said gaily; "it's a very sad position for you, I admit; but for the present you're dependent on your mother—not such a very stingy mother, eh, sir? I think you'll find it will be all right for you, when the right young woman turns up, as no doubt she will some day. Perhaps you'll find that your mother won't abdicate so very ungracefully. But, you see, it must be the right young woman!"

In spite of the laugh in it, there was a ring in the tone in which the words were spoken which was full of significance, and the significance and the laughter seemed to be doing battle together as Mrs. Romayne went on, ignoring Julian's interjection:

"I don't think you would have found it a very pleasant situation, to be engaged to Miss Newton with the prospect before you of keeping her waiting until you had made your fortune at the bar; and I'm sorry to say I don't share your conviction of the moment, that she is the right young woman. She is very pretty, I allow, and a very nice girl, no doubt." Mrs. Romayne's voice grew a little hard as she said the last words. "But she's not at all the sort of girl that I should like you to marry. She has no money, in the first place."

"I have enough for both," said Julian impetuously, and then stopped short and coloured crimson.

His mother broke into a merry laugh.

"No, poor boy!" she said. "I have enough for both! That's just what I want you to remember in your intercourse with pretty girls. After all, you know, the position has its advantages! You may flirt as much as you like while you're known to be dependent on your mother, and no one will take you too seriously."

Julian did not echo her laugh, nor did he make any comment on her words. He sat with his face turned away from her, and a rather strange expression in his eyes—an expression which was at once unformed and mutinous. His mother could not see it, but the outline of his profile apparently disturbed her. The anxiety in her face deepened again, mixed this time with an expression of doubt and self-distrust. As though to emphasize the lightness of her preceding tone, she turned the conversation into a comment on the landscape, and took up her paper again.

The remainder of the journey passed in total silence; and the drive home from the station was silent, too. An arrival in London at the end of September is not a very pleasant proceeding, unless it is approached with considerable industry, determination, and a large stock of energy. The butterflies of society, and, indeed, a large proportion of the bees, have not yet returned. Those who have returned have done so under stern compulsion to begin the winter's work; and there is a general, all-pervading sentiment as of the end of holidays and the beginning of term time.

The day that had been so radiantly lovely in Norfolk had evidently been oppressively hot and airless in town, and the general air of exhaustion and squalor, which such circumstances are apt to produce in London, did not help to render its appearance more attractive.

Number twenty-two, Queen Anne Street, Chelsea, itself seemed to be touched by the general depression. The summer flowers in the window-boxes had been taken away, and their successors were apparently waiting for orders from the mistress of the house; and as Mrs. Romayne and Julian entered the hall, there was that indefinable atmosphere about the house which two months' abandonment to even the best of servants is apt to produce—an atmosphere which is the reverse of cheerful. There were letters lying on the hall-table, one of which Mrs. Romayne handed to Julian with the comment: "From Mr. Allardyce, isn't it, Julian? Will he be ready for you to-morrow?"

Julian's legal studies were, in fact, to begin in earnest on the following day; and when, the next morning, he said good-bye to his mother and set out for the Temple, she followed him to the door with a laughing "Good speed." That, at least, was her ostensible motive, but there was something in her face as she laid her hand on his arm as he turned away on the doorstep which suggested that the last words she said to him were those that she had really followed him to say.

"What time shall you be back, Julian?"

And as he answered carelessly:

"I can't tell; not till dinner-time, I expect," there came into her eyes a curious shadow of yearning anxiety.

"Take care of yourself, sir!" she said lightly, and went back into the house.

That shadow lived in her eyes all day as she went about giving orders and "putting things to rights," as she said; striving in fact, with a concealed earnestness which seemed somewhat disproportionate to its object, to give the house that peculiar air of brightness which had been so characteristic of it, and which somehow did not seem so easily to be obtained as formerly.

Her face was gaiety itself, however, when she stood in the drawing-room as the dinner-bell rang, very daintily dressed in a tea-gown which Julian had admired, waiting for her son. A moment elapsed and Julian dashed downstairs, breathless and apologetic, but rather sparing of his words. His first day's work hardly seemed to have dissipated the cloud which had hung about him that morning at breakfast, and as his mother slipped her hand playfully into his arm with a laughing word or two of forgiveness, he turned and led her out of the room without the response which would have been natural to him.

"Have you had a pleasant day?" said Mrs. Romayne lightly, as they sat down to dinner.

"Pretty well," returned Julian indifferently. He said no more, and Mrs. Romayne, with one of her quick, half-furtive glances at him, began to talk of her own day. She had paid some calls in the afternoon, and had a great deal of news for him as to who had and who had not returned to town; and a great deal of gossip which was both amusing in itself, and rendered more amusing by the piquant animation with which she retailed it. It failed to rouse much interest in Julian, apparently, however, and after a time his mother returned to her original topic—again with a quick, anxious glance at his face.

"Did you find Mr. Allardyce easy to work with?" she enquired, interestedly this time.

"Yes: I suppose so," was the unresponsive response.

"How long did he keep you?"

"I got away at four o'clock."

Something seemed to leap in Mrs. Romayne's eyes—to be instantly suppressed—as she said, with an indifference which any ear keener than Julian's might have detected to be forced:

"Four o'clock! And what have you been doing since then, may I ask? You did not come in till a quarter past seven."

Perhaps Julian felt the inquisition in the question, though he was conscious of nothing unusual in his mother's voice; for he answered, rather briefly:

"I went to the Garrick with a fellow."

"What fellow?" demanded his mother in the same tone.

Julian moved impatiently.

"There's another fellow reading with Allardyce," he answered. "Griffiths—he took me in."

As though the suppressed impatience of his tone had not escaped her, Mrs. Romayne found herself reminded at this point of something she had heard that afternoon during one of her visits. And she proceeded to place her little piece of news before Julian with every advantage that narration could give it, though her face looked rather thin and sharp as she talked. Dinner was over by this time, and as she finished with a laugh, she rose from her seat, and put her hand on Julian's arm. His face was somewhat bored and dissatisfied, as though his mother's effort for his entertainment entirely failed to compensate him for the merry house-parties of the last month.

"I think I shall have to come and keep you company while you smoke your cigar," she said lightly; adding, with an assumption of a sudden thought on the subject which was not wholly successful: "By-the-bye, the Garrick Club must be a most attractive spot if you stayed there from four o'clock till seven?"

Julian took a quick step forward. The movement might have been due to his desire to open the door for her, or it might have been an expression of the irritation of which his face was full.

"I didn't get there at four," he said. "I really don't know what time it was, but it must have been nearly five. And I walked home; so I left somewhere about half-past six."

The irritation was in his voice as well as in his face; and his mother patted him gaily on the shoulder, with her most artificially self-deriding laugh.

"He's quite annoyed at being asked so many questions!" she exclaimed. "It's a dreadful nuisance to have such a silly old mother, isn't it? But you haven't told me what Mr. Griffiths is like yet?"

Julian had tried to laugh in answer to her first words; but the sound produced had been almost as greatly wanting in reality as had been the ease of his mother's tone, and he answered now with undisguised impatience.

"Like? Oh, he's like—any other fellow, mother. Nothing particular, one way or the other." He paused a moment, and then added hastily: "I was rather thinking of running down to the club this evening, dear, if you wouldn't mind being alone. I want to hear whether Loring has come back. There's just a chance he might be there, you know."

He had said that morning that there was no likelihood of Loring's returning for another two or three days; but Mrs. Romayne forbore to remind him of that fact. Nor did she allude to the conviction which had turned her suddenly rather pale; namely, that his thoughts of going down to the club had arisen within the last few minutes.

"Very well, dear," she said, smiling up at him. "Go, by all means. Oh, no! I shall be quite happy with a book."

He did not look back at her as he left the room after another word or two, or the expression on her face might have arrested even his youthfully self-centred and preoccupied attention.

Loring was not at the club, nor was there any information to be obtained there as to his movements. Julian played a game of billiards and lost it through sheer carelessness, and then determined to go home again. He would walk part of the way, he said to himself, though he had had one walk that day. He wanted to "think things over."

The phrase was serious, and by comparison with the process to which it was attached, grandiloquent. Julian's mental apparatus was at present as undeveloped as that of a fashionable young man of four-and-twenty may usually be taken to be. The process of "thinking things over," as conducted within his good-looking head, involved no stern process of reasoning, no exhaustive system of logical deduction from cause to effect, no carefully-balanced opinions of the past or decisions for the future. When he proposed to himself to "think things over," in short, he simply meant that he should ring a strictly limited number of changes on the fact that, as he expressed it vaguely to himself, it was "awfully hard lines."

It had taken him some time to come to this conclusion. He had flirted with Miss Hilda Newton very happily for the last ten days, with a great deal of wholly unnecessary assistance from that young lady herself, without the very faintest definite intentions towards her. He had enjoyed it, and she had enjoyed it; and the idea which had occurred to him once or twice, that his mother did not enjoy it, had not particularly affected him. Circumstances alone would have been responsible for the proposal which had so nearly been an accomplished fact on the day before. And had the speech to Miss Newton, interrupted by Mrs. Romayne, reached its legitimate conclusion, and received its inevitable response, it was extremely likely that he might by this time have been the victim of a vague consciousness of having made a mistake. But it had been interrupted; and a deeply-injured sense of having been thwarted was consequently not unnatural in its author. That sense of injury which might have passed away in mere sentiment, but which, on the other hand, might, if it had been left untouched by words, have developed into a secret breach between mother and son, had been focussed and rendered definite and tangible, as it were, by his mother's laughing speeches in the train. It was as he had sat gazing blankly out of the window during the last half-hour of their journey, that he had come to the conclusion before mentioned that it was "awfully hard lines."

"It makes a fellow feel such a fool!" he said to himself as morosely as the undeveloped nature of his temperament permitted, as he issued moodily from his club and started in the direction of Piccadilly. "It makes a fellow feel such a confounded fool!" He could not reduce this general principle to detail, but what he really felt was something of the sensation of the child who realises suddenly and for the first time the "pretence" of the fairyland of shadows in which he has been performing prodigies of valour.

All the intercourse with the pretty girls of his "sets" which Julian had hitherto accepted simply and unquestioningly, had suddenly become flat, stale, and unprofitable to him. All illusions had gone from it, and the reality was painfully unsatisfying, and wounding to his self-love. There is all the difference in the world between a vague understanding and a practical realisation. Julian had known, of course, from the very first that he was dependent on his mother, but he had never felt it until the previous day. He had known that marriage without her consent was practically impossible for him; but the fact had never before been brought home to him. The veto which had descended so impalpably and decisively upon what he was now prepared to characterise as his hopes, with regard to Miss Newton, shrivelling them to nothingness, had also shrivelled away all the embellishing haze by which the conditions of his life had been surrounded.

The background to all his thoughts on the subject; the background which had grown up almost without consciousness on his own part, with his first humiliated realisation of the facts of the case, and which remained a vague, brooding shadow in his mind; was resentment against his mother; a resentment which, taken in conjunction with the careless and effusive affection of his attitude to her hitherto, threw a curious light on his relations with her. But against this background, and affecting him far more keenly, was a sore sense that life had suddenly lost its savour for him. The charm of flirtation had vanished utterly before his mother's words as to its harmlessness. The privilege which she assigned to him seemed to reduce him to the level of a shadow among substances, to put him at a hopeless disadvantage with all the women of his world, and render his intercourse with them a farce of which both they and he must be perfectly conscious.

"It's all such utter humbug!" he said to himself, that being the nearest definition he could attain of the vague thoughts that were passing through his mind. Then he ceased to express himself, even mentally, and walked along, meditating moodily and discontentedly. He was walking along Piccadilly when he found his thoughts gradually returning to his actual surroundings as though something were drawing them, unconsciously to himself, as extraneous objects which one is not even aware of noticing will sometimes do.

It was about eleven o'clock: not a very pleasant time in Piccadilly; and the pavement was by no means crowded. The first detail to which he awoke was the hilarious demeanour of a young man just in front of him, who was walking, very unsteadily, in the same direction as himself. He was a young man of the commonest cockney type, obviously in the maudlin stage of intoxication.

As Julian's senses became more fully alive he noticed, a pace or two in front of the young man, the shabbily-dressed figure of a girl. She was walking hurriedly and nervously, and as the young man quickened his uneven steps in response to a sudden quickening of hers, Julian saw that the intoxicated speeches which had first grown into his own meditation were addressed to the girl, and that she was trying in vain to escape from them. It was not a particularly uncommon sight for a London street, and a half-indignant, half-careless glance would naturally have been all the attention Julian would have vouchsafed it. But as the pair preceded him up Piccadilly; the girl shrinking and afraid; afraid to attract attention by too rapid movements; as much afraid, as her nervous, undecided glances around her showed, of the help a protest might attract to her as of her pursuer; the man, sodden and brutal, absolutely destitute for the moment of reasoning faculty; Julian found his attention fascinated by them.

A spark of natural youthful chivalry, entirely undeveloped by his life, stirred in him. He quickened his steps, involuntarily apparently, and with no definite intention, for he was just passing them with a quick, undecided glance at the girl, when he saw her stop suddenly and shrink back against a neighbouring shop-front. Whether a faint shriek really came from her, or not, he never knew, but her eyes met his and appealed to him almost as if without the owner's consciousness. The man had laid a hot, drunken hand upon the worn, ungloved fingers.

Julian stopped.

"Let go!" he said peremptorily. His tone was so sharp, and the interference was so sudden and unlooked-for, that the man, stupid with drink, did as he was bidden as if involuntarily. "Be off!" continued Julian in the same tone.

The man stared at him for a minute, and broke into a maudlin laugh, a discordant snatch of a comic song, and staggered on his way, as though the sudden breaking of his chain of ideas had obliterated the girl from his memory.

She was standing, as Julian turned to her, leaning back against the shop-front, shaking from head to foot, but evidently making a violent effort to control herself.

"Thank you, sir," she murmured tremulously, and was moving to go on her way with faltering, trembling footsteps, when Julian stopped her.

"This is not a nice place for you to be alone in," he said almost involuntarily. "Have you far to go?"

He had looked at her for that moment during which she had stood motionless, with her face outlined against the dark shutter, with a strangely mingled feeling that her face was wonderfully unlike any with which he was acquainted; and yet that he had actually seen it before—seen it, and experienced the same half-startled, half-wondering sensation. It was white now to the very lips, and the great, brown eyes, dark and liquid, looked out from under their soft lashes and level eyebrows, wide with terror and distress. Her features were beautifully formed, though they were so thin and worn that it would never have occurred to Julian to class her among the ranks of pretty girls. But the real charm of her face lay about her mouth. It was very strong—though the strength was latent and entirely unconscious; very simple, and very sweet; and even the pallor of her lips and the slight trembling about them could not detract from the beauty of the line they made. Her hair, as Julian noticed, was of a soft black and very luxuriant. She was rather tall, and her shabby jacket concealed and spoilt the outline of her figure; but the set of her well-shaped head was full of instinctive grace.

She paused a moment before she answered him, looking into his face with a simple directness which had a dignity of its own.

"Yes, sir," she said in a low voice, which shook a little in spite of her evident efforts to steady it; "to the Hammersmith Road."

"But you're not going to walk, are you?" said Julian.

Apparently her glance at his face had satisfied her. She answered him this time without hesitation.

"Yes, sir," she said.

Her voice was very musical and refined. It harmonised better with her face than with her worn, work-girl's dress, and the dignified deference of her manner.

"Then you must let me see you safely part of the way, at any rate," said Julian impulsively.

She hesitated, and looked at him again, and this time the large eyes grew moist with tears.

"It's very silly of me," she said tremulously. "I—I think it was his touching me that upset me so."

She had been rubbing one hand, all this time, mechanically and involuntarily, as it seemed, over the hand on which that drunken touch had fallen.

"I did try to get a 'bus, but they were all full. I couldn't let you take such trouble."

It needed only the unconscious gratitude of those words to convince Julian that it would be no trouble whatever. And he asserted the same with an assumption of authority and masterfulness quite new to him.

It was an hour and a half later when his mother, sitting up, wakeful, in her own room, caught the slight sound made by his latch-key in the door, and noticed a moment's pause before the door was opened. In that pause there had come to Julian one of those sudden flashes of light which sometimes illuminate a vainly-pondered question.

"Of course!" he said to himself, as he shut the door with a bang. "Of course! I knew I'd seen her before! In the thunderstorm, the night I dined with Garstin!"

END OF VOL. I

Milton Keynes UK
Ingram Content Group UK Ltd.
UKHW030742071024
449371UK00006B/631